THE PRAGMATIC PRESIDENCY

THE
PRAGMATIC
PRESIDENCY

Effective Leadership
In The Two-Year College

Edwin E. Vineyard, Ed.D.
President-Emeritus
Northern Oklahoma College

Anker Publishing Company, Inc.
Bolton, MA

THE PRAGMATIC PRESIDENCY
Effective Leadership In The Two-Year College

ISBN 0-9627042-4-5

Composition by Jim Wehtje.
Cover Design by Marianna Montuori.

Anker Publishing Company, Inc.
176 Ballville Road
P.O. Box 249
Bolton, MA 01740-0249

DEDICATION

to the author's son

Dr. Edwin R. Vineyard

who has chosen to follow the path of junior college instruction
and who exemplifies characteristics for future leadership
in this significant tier of institutions of higher education

Who is the happy Warrior? Who is he
That every man in arms should wish to be?
'Tis he whose law is reason; who depends
Upon that law as on the best of friends;
Who with a natural instinct to discern
What knowledge can perform, is diligent to learn.
Who, if he rise to station of command,
Rises by open means; and there to stand
On honorable terms, or else retire,
And in himself possess his own desire.
Who comprehends his trust, and to the same
Keeps faithful with a singleness of aim.
And, through the heat of conflict, keeps the law
In calmness made, and sees what he foresaw.
Plays, in the many games of life, that one
Where what he most doth value must be won;
Whom neither shape of danger can dismay,
Nor thought of tender happiness betray.
This is the happy Warrior; this is He
That every Man in arms should wish to be.

(excerpted from William Wordsworth's *The Happy Warrior*)

ABOUT THE AUTHOR

Edwin E. Vineyard recently retired after spending twenty-five years as president of Northern Oklahoma College, a state institution in Tonkawa since 1901. During his tenure the college emerged from the shadow of accrediting probation and other difficulties to become one of the recognized centers of quality among two-year colleges in the region. His institution has been in the forefront of sound innovations and enduring change within the state.

Dr. Vineyard has been the recipient of a number of honors and awards, including the Transformational Leadership Award from the University of Texas, a resolution of honor from his state legislature, the setting aside of a day in his honor by proclamation of the Oklahoma governor, and a "Bravo" from the area public broadcasting network.

The author's educational leadership positions include service on both the initial task force and the commission on small/rural community colleges of the American Association of Community and Junior Colleges. He has served as a consultant-examiner, commissioner, and as a chairman of evaluation teams for the North Central Association for more than twenty years. Within the state he has served several terms as chairman of the Junior College Presidents and as chairman of the Council of College and University Presidents. In a consulting role, he designed and directed a Kellogg-sponsored research project on adult education in Oklahoma. Dr. Vineyard has served as president of the state's higher education association and personnel association. He has been chairman of the state's education and public television board and the state's Advisory Committee on Mental Health. In private business, he has been chairman of a bank board and of the board for Oklahoma Blue Cross and Blue Shield.

The author's educational experience includes a stint as a secondary school teacher and principal, professor and counseling director in a four-year university, professor, division head, and personnel dean in a five-year university, and professor and director of graduate studies in a college within a comprehensive university. He has published both opinion and research articles in major journals and is the coauthor of The *Profession of Teaching*. Dr. Vineyard has also written a chapter on personnel practices for the *Handbook on Community College Administration*.

Dr. Vineyard married Imogene Mankin in 1946. They have had two sons, Louis (deceased) and Edwin, the latter serving on the faculty of Northern Oklahoma College with his wife, Susan.

CONTENTS

FOREWORD

My colleague, Ed Vineyard, has done in this book what many of us in the community college field plan to do and talk about doing, but never have the self-discipline to accomplish. In doing so, he has made a significant contribution to the literature of his chosen field.

There is an old saying about the recipe for making rabbit stew—first, you catch a rabbit! Applied to this situation, the prelude to advising people and sharing experiences with them is to have some in-depth experiences over an extended period of time which positions you to have something worth sharing. Ed Vineyard has done this and has thereby earned himself a place on the podium from which practitioners and would-be practitioners may anticipate some worthwhile, usable advice.

As a toiler in the vineyard (no pun intended), I don't agree with all of the conclusions reached by the author. In fact, his coverage is so all-inclusive that no one I've ever known would agree with all of the amazingly large number of topics on which judgments are made. Ed is a philosophic guy who is serious about understanding why things are the way they are, and is willing to work to find out. He is also a get-the-job-done kind of person who doesn't back off until the philosophy has been implemented and something good has happened. Some twenty-five years ago he abandoned the university lectern to assume the helm of a moderate-sized junior college in a basically rural area. It has been in this setting that he has hawked his wares for the past quarter-century. He has compiled a superior professional record and retired from a college which reflects this exemplary leadership.

This work is a most unusual example of combining clearly articulated philosophic positions with how-to-do-it advice. I wish I had had a copy of this book when I assumed my first junior college presidency. I had access to a great deal of written material, but it was scattered among many sources. Ed has brought it together in one volume and presented it in a coherent, meaningful form, enriched by references to professional experiences which validate conclusions and recommendations.

In conclusion, I believe that Dr. Vineyard has indeed enriched the professional literature of the community college field, and I commend the book to both active practitioners and those who are considering a career in the junior college field.

Bill J. Priest, Chancellor-Emeritus
Dallas County Community College District

PREFACE

This is a book about the two-year college presidency. It is written for practicing presidents, new presidents, and aspiring presidents. It is written for trustees and all others who seek in a scholarly way to understand the nature of the presidency, and the purview and purlieu of that office. It is written for all who seek an information base for effective interaction with those who occupy the presidency. It will serve also as a means of gaining insight into the inner psychological and emotional press of the presidency upon those who bear these responsibilities of leadership.

This is, first and foremost, a practical guide to the presidency and its various functions. It approaches the presidency by examining the essence of the position. It then shifts to offer extensive coverage of the search process for new presidents, both from the standpoint of the institution and the aspirants. It discusses presidential transitions and the effects of these on colleges undergoing leadership changes. It is a rarity to find treatment of these topics and perspectives under one cover, and this has been a challenge to the writer.

The text continues with identification of the various constituencies with which the president must work, and discussions of interaction modes and techniques with each of these. The subject of college governance, both internal and external, is explored. The different facets of institutional operations are highlighted, with practical ideas and suggestions. Personnel policies and practices receive special attention because of the complexity and the significance attributed to this vital area. Institutional research and planning are discussed from rationale to execution.

This is perhaps the only text of its kind to give extensive treatment to various aspects of the president's service environment, such as perquisites and performance evaluation, as well as providing a discussion of the most recent thrusts in accreditation involving assessment and evaluation of learning outcomes. The book has special meanings and applications within the non-urban community college sector, and thus is unique in including a chapter on this most numerous version of two-year institutions.

For those with interest in the practical administrative problems faced week-to-week and month-to-month by active presidents, there is a section providing some sixty case situations for review. These should prove valuable learning and discussion exercises for graduate seminars and workshops, as well as for practitioners in the field.

This book has been written at the behest of numerous friends and colleagues in higher education, and in junior colleges in particular, who have generously credited the writer with laurels of leadership, some skill in expression, and a richness of experience from which others might profit. After a short respite in retirement, following twenty-five years at the presidential helm, stirrings from within gained the intensity of compulsive urges. I knew that I must undertake the preparation of a book in which could be shared some of the more significant accumulated knowledge and understandings about the presidency. This must be a practical source, although not without an ideological base. It must be direct, forthright, and candid. It must avoid neither the personal aspects of the presidency nor the effects of the presidency upon the person. Being a president is an intensely personal experience, and this must not be crowded or covered by extensive reference and deference to the scholarly works of others. It must not hesitate to postulate dogma where appropriate.

Throughout this book the president is referenced with pronouns of the masculine gender. The author hastens to state in advance that the presidency is clearly an office appropriately occupied and aspired toward by persons of both genders. The choice of the masculine form defers to custom, and is one of convenience only, thus avoiding the redundancy and awkwardness of double references.

The writer acknowledges the lifelong support of his first lady, Imogene, and encouragement of his family, Ed and Susan, as well as good friends, in this endeavor. The assistance of Dr. Joe A. Leone, former chancellor of the Oklahoma State System of Higher Education, who made suggestions and offered encouragement, is acknowledged. The writer gives special thanks to Dr. Bill J. Priest, a greatly admired former colleague president and chancellor of the Dallas County Community College System, for his willingness to write the foreword. The writer's son, who represents the future of the profession and to whom the book is dedicated, has been a consistent inspiration to his father.

A work of this nature is revealing of the background and personality of the writer. The two-year college experience of the writer has been in a non-urban college, and this perspective cannot but come through in the text. Perhaps also the writer's background in four-year and graduate universities will reveal itself in respect for academic traditions. For the new generation of leaders, may this text provide a boost toward new professional frontiers.

Edwin E. Vineyard
President-Emeritus
Northern Oklahoma College

PART ONE

The Presidency in Transition

THE NATURE
OF THE PRESIDENCY

1

P erhaps there is no satisfactory approach to describing the nature of the collegiate presidency. Each reader brings to the term certain meanings, some of which may be personal but most of which have some commonality with others in higher education. Probably no single approach is adequate. A simple description of duties is insufficient. Even a cataloging and discussion of roles is not enough. Utilizing the cumulative expectancies of constituencies within the higher education sphere tends to present an unbalanced image.

This chapter looks at the presidency first in terms of what some have called its *aura*. If that nebulous quality could be captured in words, it would be sufficient to set the collegiate presidency apart from all other leadership positions, inside or outside of higher education. To date no writer has succeeded in this effort. Nevertheless, any substantive attempt to define the presidency must begin in terms of its aura, moving on to provide descriptions of central roles and leadership styles. That is the approach which follows.

Although most of this book centers on the presidency, and thus attempts to provide a broad operational definition of the position, this chapter makes a vain attempt to capsulize the quintessence of the position.

THE AURA

Some writers have referred to the *mystique* of the presidency, while others have used the term *aura* to describe that special quality that separates this office from all others in the institution. Where there is no aura or mystique, there is no *presidency* as such. This may be considered a strong statement, but it is a thought that deserves careful consideration by aspiring or new presidents. Without it the president is simply the chief manager, the department head of administration, or a colleague with an elevated title and salary. Each of these has a noticeable difference in connotation, perception, and value level from that which is associated with *president* or *leader*.

The etiology of the concept of the mystique of the president is possibly as curious as the concept itself. It may be that popular literature and drama have led to the attribution of this special quality. The portrayal of the liberal arts college presidency by Ronald Coleman in the *Halls of Ivy* series may have added a dimension to this common perception. If so, the portrayals in certain of the Disney movies would tend to be offsetting. It is more likely a holdover from the experiences and traditions of the years prior to the 1960s. Kauffman (1980) tends to present the presidency as an evolving position, greatly influenced and changed by events and trends occurring during the last quarter-century.

Whatever the origin of the notion of the aura, it tends to shroud even the most common of those who are named to this high education office. Its character and depth will tend to depend somewhat upon the conduct of the predecessors in the particular presidency, and most certainly the quality of this nebulous ambience, as well as its continuity and its usefulness, will depend heavily upon the conduct and style of the inheritor of the mantle.

Perhaps the most common error of judgment made by new presidents is to approach the position with the notion that the way to lead is to be one of the group. Nothing closes the distance between the president and the staff so quickly, and nothing destroys the ability to lead during stress, or on a permanent basis, so fast. This speaks also to the greater difficulty of the insider named as president in establishing a presidential charisma.

The president must convey the desire to be considered as a professional colleague, but as a colleague who is different, not only because he (generic pronoun) occupies a different position, has broader concerns, and is better informed about these broader institutional concerns, but also because he must be the leader. The president must convey a personal interest in every program and every department while retaining and declaring a need for a broader perspective. The president must convey a personal interest in each member of the staff from custodian to dean, without making himself vulnerable to any. He must develop a personal relationship with many, yet never bare himself fully to any. He must open himself momentarily for glimpses as a person, but never for an extended view.

There is nothing inherently wrong if staff and students at times wonder if indeed this person puts on his trousers (or other apparel) in precisely the same fashion as others, and certainly no one should be knowledgeable for sure. It is well to explain decisions and actions, but is not necessary to explain all the reasons nor to convey the notion of direct accountability. But one must consistently convey truthfully from these explanations that actions are taken for reasons related to the welfare of the institution and its constituent groups.

Perhaps the discussion above may suggest artificiality, snobbery, or benevolent despotism. Such is not the intent and would, of course, be a fatal error. The president must be ready and willing to interact on a limited basis with both individuals and groups within the institution in a candid and honest fashion. But he must retain in his bearing that he is not interacting as an equal, but as one who must in most cases bear the burden of responsibility for the outcomes. Infrequent open agonizing and travail over difficult and unpopular decisions may not hurt his leadership status, but cautions must be observed. All decisions must be made firmly and with confidence when matters reach that stage.

The president must retain some personal and psychological distance from all staff, although forming somewhat closer bonding with his administrative team. This distance is necessary to his leadership role. It is also necessary to the maintenance of his own mental health. Since the president must evaluate those who serve beneath him, presumably in an objective manner, and since on occasion his recommendation may be for demotion or discharge, he cannot afford close friendships. This is not to suggest that friendships kept on a professional level are inappropriate, but rather that "buddy" relationships can be a problem.

This leads to another point. While power over others should never be entrusted to anyone who does not have compassion, making difficult decisions which are personally injurious to others can be stressful to a caring president. Nevertheless, duty to the institution must be fulfilled. One must simply be certain of the right decision, then live with the consequences. These will take their toll internally over time, but the president must never become callous about matters which affect people. The caring president must and should agonize within himself when his decisions adversely affect the lives of others. This is the price he pays. But he must make the tough decisions, and it must be known that he makes these and not others beneath him.

An essential feature of the aura surrounding the presidency is the perception of this office as the champion of the institution, its staff, and its students. The president must be perceived as ready to mount his white charger and go off to joust with bureaucrats, politicians, and others to win the cause for the college. He does not have to be successful in all efforts, but it helps if he wins a few battles. Nothing solidifies a group as much as having some common enemies. The president must be seen standing up to pressure groups, state boards or executives, and others who would seek to make changes which are not in the best interest of the college and its constituencies.

Aura has something to do also with the image projected. The president, and the spouse, must consciously project and protect the proper image of the presidential office. This must be an image with basic dignity and culture, with a few spontaneous revelations of the real people who occupy the position. This not a suggestion of a "regal" presidency, but it must have some hint of this.

There are some things presidents do and do not do in public and in their relations with others. Even clothing is important. Colleagues should wonder at times if the president sleeps in a suit, although there may be a few occasions when he proves that this uniform is not a part of his body. While the president should relate to colleagues, board members, and constituents in an easy, friendly, and sometimes joking manner, there must be a line which is not crossed in familiarity or conduct. Otherwise, the mystique is lost, and his effectiveness is diminished.

There is the possibility of another facet of the aura which is seldom discussed, probably because it is certain to be controversial in the current climate. This is intimidation. The aura may be, in and of its own, somewhat intimidating. Authority is an intimidating characteristic.

The president needs to understand these truths, and may take steps to alter this quality in degree but never in essence. That is, he must accept the mild form of intimidation which accompanies his position of authority, and the aura it holds, as a leadership tool rather than a handicap. Similarly, he must make certain that this quality does not become excessive, for this would be deleterious to the total psychological and social climate, and thus to the teaching-learning environment.

Fisher (1984) discusses the concept of aura under the term charisma. He notes that sincerity, appearance, goodness, confidence, wisdom, courage, thoughtfulness, kindness, and control are all contributing factors. But he declares that the most important attributes are distance, style, and perceived self confidence. Of these three, he sees distance as the most significant. Others (Vaughan, 1989) have spoken about the presidential platform, and have stressed the need for maintaining position on that platform at all times.

Vaughan (1989) cautions presidents about taking advice to be distant too seriously, pointing to the circumstances in some institutions which cry out for a president willing to establish intimacy within the college. He approaches the concept of distance in terms of "one step back," suggesting that the president should rarely be the first point of contact for a problem within the college. He stresses the significance of effective delegation of responsibility for first response. Most caution that distance is not to be confused with aloofness. Fisher suggests that the president be a "friendly phantom" darting in and out of college affairs, but not remaining long enough anywhere to become familiar to others.

Both Fisher and Vaughan caution presidents against accepting roles and assignments within the civic community which bog them down in time and energy, and which are roles which should be occupied by persons of lower rank than the president. Fisher cautions presidents about participating as one of the group in on-campus committee and council meetings. He urges presidents to make an appearance, state a position if appropriate, then to leave. This contributes to distance. He states also that charismatic leadership can best be exercised in structured circumstances.

Different writers have cautioned presidents about intimate or close relationships with individual faculty members. Some include other administrators in this advice. The basic rationale for such advice borders on the "familiarity breeds contempt" notion, although it centers on the idea that close relationships tend to reveal weaknesses as well as strengths, and that even perceived strengths are diminished under such circumstances of knowing too much about the president. Presidents are cautioned not to reveal to anyone their own self-doubts and personal fears. Fisher suggests that if the president is to let down and talk to anyone, it should be a loyal and trustworthy assistant whose only job is to assist the president.

One disadvantage of having persons on the staff who have a close relationship with the president is that these may feel more open in discussing presidential decisions and discouraging risk-taking behaviors, which are necessary but often criticized by others internally. A corollary to this point is that having others close enough to relay criticisms, second-guess decisions in conversations with the president, and generally serve as conscience spokespersons, may tend to undermine the president's confidence in his own decisions. This may lead to tentativeness in decision making, and an unconscious urge to please friends. Nothing could be more disastrous to a president.

It is important that a president exude a self-confident image on campus, and externally as well. The staff must perceive that the president is a confident person who knows what he is doing as their leader. The president must behave, and he must speak, with confidence. He must be poised, not easily rattled. He must even walk confidently. People must see in him a confidence that the college's problems can be met and solved. They must perceive him as being able to meet any problem or challenge which may come the institution's way.

Of course, being confident is of great assistance in acting confident. The president can ill afford those around him who do not contribute something to his self-confidence. For this reason, having intimate friends who are willing to tell him regularly what he is doing wrong is not a helpful situation for a president. Of course, this is not to say that there may not be value in getting honestly critical opinions on occasion, but as a rule the president receives a sufficient amount of these from adversaries. The point is that while one cannot afford to overlook contrary opinion and evidence, basically the president must believe that what he is doing is correct and that the decisions he makes are the best ones in the light of available information. He cannot afford to be overly analytical and self-scrutinizing; he must be confident in his own judgments and follow them through.

As a part of his aura, the president must be seen as visionary. Every president must have a vision for the institution which may be described in intellectual terms, but is calculated to stir emotions. It must be constantly articulated, both on and off campus. This vision need not, and should not, be tedious in detail, nor should it be one which is constantly shifting. The presidential vision should be broad and sweeping in its scope, a statement of the high principles which will guide the institution's development. The details will be filled in from time to time as conditions are altered, but the vision will remain consistent. In order for charismatic leadership to occur, there must be an acceptance of this vision among college constituencies, along with an added emotional concomitant.

Every president has his own style. Because of personality differences, it is difficult for one president to adopt the style of another, even that of a mentor or a much-admired colleague. While each president must adopt his own style, in order to be successful the style must be presidential. It is a mistake to believe that one has the personal qualities which will enable breaking with the traditions, the findings of research, and the wisdom of those who have occupied positions of presidential leadership successfully over the years. Every president must define an image which he will in all his roles seek to depict.

IDENTIFICATION

Louis XIV of France is supposed to have said, "I am the State." He was also quite a proponent of the "divine right" of kings to govern. While no one would be foolish enough to propose any divine rights for presidents, a certain level of personal identification with the institution is appropriate and necessary to presidential motivation and success. Any president must, of course, understand that the institution is far greater, and much more significant, than any single person. Nevertheless, the intensely motivated president will tend to identify himself and the institution.

This identity syndrome can be both healthy and unhealthy, for not only the institution but for the person as well. Such a president will take criticisms of the institution, or any facet within it, as personal. This, in turn, tends to provoke a defensiveness on his part.

The identity pattern leads to greater personal stress on the occupant of the presidential office. His responses may tend to be more emotional and less rational. He may be defensive to criticisms which should be taken as constructive, and from which the institution might profit through change.

Similarly, the identity syndrome may lead to the president taking more credit than he deserves from the good things which may be transpiring. He may bask in favorable publicity for accomplishments with which he had little to do. A president must accept such recognition gracefully, acknowledge it, and then share the credit magnanimously (and perhaps correctly) with those who have contributed. Nevertheless, since the president is often blamed for things which are not under his direct control, he must indeed take whatever credit may be due to the incubator climate which his leadership has created in making the successes possible.

It has been said that the institution is merely the lengthened shadow of one man. It is instead the shadow silhouette of many people who contribute to its character and its work. In accepting recognition which is due, the president must avoid excessive pride and egocentrism.

While the consequences of an exaggerated identification with the institution may be many, these may be preferable to the lack of any such feeling or emotion. While self-aggrandizement should be avoided, that which is reflected from the glories of the college itself are welcomed. A president cannot be objective, aloof, or emotionally distanced from his institution. He must care about the college intensely, even above and beyond his own career goals and personal happiness.

Another way of describing the identity syndrome, albeit a distorted one, is that of proprietorship. It is said that some presidents act as if they owned the place. It has been said that some presidents are so tight with the purse strings that it appears they think it is their own money being spent. Identification, as it is used in the context of this writing does not connote a sense of proprietorship. Instead it suggests a personal relationship of self and college based upon loyalty, dedication, and intense professionalism with an added emotional component.

It is also true that often the general public tends to identify the college with the president, especially when the president has had long tenure. Policies, procedures, and decisions, regardless of what office or group may have made them, tend to be attributed to the president. Some subordinates may contribute to this notion either intentionally or in their manner.

It is very difficult to assign real responsibility or accountability elsewhere. The president tends to be held accountable, and perhaps this is as it should be. But accountability without the authority to act decisively is inappropriate for the titular head of any enterprise. A president who has been given broad authority to administer and to make decisions, including those pertaining to personnel, must expect to be held accountable. However, the president who has only limited authority over personnel and internal affairs can assume only that degree of responsibility which is his own.

A president is justified in believing that the institution would not be the same without him. If indeed he is exercising leadership, or if he is failing to do so, this would tend to be the case. It is a function of the president to set a tone for the college, and thus the institution tends to reflect this to the degree that he is successful in so doing.

ROLES OF THE PRESIDENT

Pedantry in the form of a litany of duties and responsibilities of the president seems inappropriate for the purposes of the sophisticated reader. Likewise, some of the more humorous writings, well-conceived and all too true, on the varied expectations made of the president seem a bit light for inclusion. Nevertheless, the role of the president is often operationally defined in practice in terms of expectations or demands, as significant as the job description in the policy and procedures manual may be.

The terms *administrator* and *manager* are often used, as is the term *chief executive officer*. The president's role includes all these, but each is inadequate. This writer tends to be offended by the term manager, although admittedly much of the president's time and energies are consumed in management type activities. Manager is a business term which connotes fiscal affairs, manipulation of people for the corporate good, and making decisions among opposing sets of facts and figures. It fails to connote leadership, although leadership skills evidently are involved in modern management theory.

Presidents often state their open opposition to being "reduced" to managers, and this has been a perceptible and growing trend during the last two decades. This implies a loss of freedom to determine the parameters within which judgments and decisions are to be made, and it implies a loss of change initiative characteristic of true leadership.

The encroachment of legal restraints, exertion of controls by the bureaucracy above, the advent of formal bargaining, and the highly detailed policy and procedures manual necessary to functioning in the current milieu, have all contributed to changing the role of the president toward the managerial image. While such change may be inevitable, presidents have an obligation to do battle to preserve the vestiges of leadership which remain.

The president may be held responsible for everything which transpires within the institution, therefore it behooves him to know what it is that is going on in all sectors. Even though the president delegates duties to others, it is very difficult to delegate responsibility. Even though a subordinate assumes both duties and responsibility for these, the transfer of the latter is seldom perfected. This is, unfortunately, the nature of public business, and to some extent corporate business as well. It is only a matter of time until the president who delegates and forgets finds himself in trouble.

The president, and sometimes the governing board chairperson, serves as spokesperson for the college. The public should hear as though a single voice came from the institution. Of course, this does not mean that the president may not allow others with specific assignments the freedom to discuss those with the public, of course. Nor does it preclude the president authorizing another to speak on general institutional policy on specific occasions and about specific matters. But, at worst, the voice heard by the public should be that of an harmonic chorus on matters of general significance.

The president is leader of the administrative team. This must be true, even though he may be the latest arrival and had no influence over their selection. It is grossly unfair and unprofessional for an incoming president to insist on choosing his administrative team in the manner of a university head football coach. Similarly, members of an administrative team have an obligation to conduct themselves as members of a unitary team unless professional conscience or legalities are violated. A team member who finds themself completely ill at ease with the president's approach should ultimately seek a change of assignment. The president must not be hesitant about dismissing or demoting a person who demonstrates that he is not a willing member of the unitary team. Neither disloyalty nor tendencies to lead in different directions from the charted course are acceptable.

The president, of course, has an obligation to recognize the special expertise of his staff in their various assignments and to avail himself of their candid advice. Administrators should never be treated as "gofers" for the president, but deserve the same professional respect as suggested elsewhere for the faculty.

The president may find himself filling voids. Any assignment which remains undelegated belongs to the president unless he delegates it. Any set of tasks not performed by the position with defined responsibility will tend to gravitate back to the president unless he takes corrective action. Some administrative team members may be quite accomplished with some tasks and not competent with others. If this is a valued person, the president often finds himself filling the void. The writer has on different occasions found himself with roles in business management, student affairs, academic deanship, and even news writing.

Versatility is a desirable attribute for a president, but it may be preferable to alter the administrative chart and definition of duties slightly to accommodate the personal attributes of valued administrative staff members. By this means the strengths of one may supplement the weaknesses of another. It is more important to adjust the chart and assignments of people in order to obtain optimum functioning than it is to maintain the sanctity of a neat organizational chart with logical perfection.

A role which the president must play on occasion is that of "parent protector" or "judge arbiter." Just as the president is the champion for the institution externally, so is he the champion internally for the weak and the downtrodden. The president rights the wrongs and corrects the injustices as revealed.

Any president, or other administrator, who takes an arbitrary position that a subordinate is always right, and always backs that person, is a fool and will soon be found out. Other things being equal, it is indeed good policy to back the decisions of subordinates. However, when a decision is appealed to the president, he must make his own judgment as to the propriety of that decision. The decision on appeal becomes his own. He cannot ratify a bad decision; he must correct it. Of course, if possible he must do so in a manner which allows the subordinate to save face.

The role of "judge-arbiter" can be a very delicate one, particularly if it involves two or more professional colleagues who have had an emotional confrontation. Since it is often difficult to discern who is right and who is wrong, the best (and usually the most correct) position is that both are wrong, and to insist that the matter be settled on a basis different than that proposed by either.

By no means should the president take sides between two strong and valuable colleagues, unless there is clear evidence of right and wrong in his own judgment. Even then, it may be best for this to emerge from further enforced discussion between the parties involved. But the president must often insist that an important matter actually be resolved, acting as an arbiter or proposing a solution unpopular with both as an incentive for further negotiation between the parties.

EXERCISING LEADERSHIP

It is uncertain whether leadership style is a conscious and studied decision of presidents, or whether the adoption of a style is the natural extension of the personality, beliefs, and value system of the individual president. It is likely that educational leadership style is determined by the interaction of a number of different factors. Among these are: (1) the personal characteristics of the leader himself; (2) the characteristics of the various constituencies internal and external to the institution; and (3) the circumstances under which initial leadership is undertaken, and the changing circumstances in which it is continued. However, once a leadership style is established and successful, it tends to be perpetuated through role perceptions and role portrayal among those most closely involved.

The president must have a primary constituency with which he identifies, even though he must interact successfully with all constituencies. As will be seen in later discussions, the writer believes that the president's primary constituency is the faculty itself. This identity should not be difficult for the president to attain within himself, since it is probable that he came from that group. Broad scholarly skills and recognition as a teacher-scholar assist in this perception by others.

The role image of a caring, student-oriented, scholarly instructor is an honorable one. It does the president no harm in his relations with students, the board, or the public. The president builds upon this perception by enlarging it to include management skills, knowledge of politics, practical planning, legal expertise, and financial acumen. But he never forgets his primary identity. First credibility will tend to come, and if he is both fortunate and successful in his role, trust will eventually follow.

Both Kauffman (1980) and Vaughan (1986) have pointed to the loneliness of the presidency. Neither the advice above regarding an identification with the faculty, nor similar advice to be offered later, should be taken too literally. The president cannot really be a member of any group. The president is a group of one. The office which he occupies demands that it be so. Effective leadership in that office requires that it be singular and apart from all other constituencies, even that of administration.

The president must maintain a certain level of control within the institution. This "control" may be over processes which are at least in part democratic. Nevertheless, the president must have that certain level of control, even while he is being purposively democratic. This is a subtlety which both the president and others must understand. This does not mean that he is manipulative, but rather that he is purposive in relinquishing and sharing authority.

Honesty is always a good policy, as is candor. Authority is not a four-letter word, and acting with authority is necessary on occasion. Public junior colleges were never designed as pure democracies, and no one should realistically expect these to be so. The president always wins tests of power when these occur, if he expects to remain successful, although he should take caution about provoking such tests. It is best if he is perceived as winning because he is right. But the president must remember that his power depends upon its rational and proper exercise. A president who abuses the power of office will soon lose it.

A president may utilize both positives and negatives in the exercise of leadership. The trappings of his office include the ability to reward and the ability to punish. However, the emphasis should not be upon actually demonstrating a system of rewards and punishments as it is upon leaving the possibility for such open in the minds of others. Intrinsics are likely more important in academia than extrinsics. Positives are generally more effective than negatives. It is always wise to be cautious about stating threats, since sometimes it is necessary to follow through with actions. The president must not be hesitant to act when the situation merits strong action.

The president must be seen as the champion of the institution and its constituencies in the political and regulatory arena and in certain other external relationships. No one respects an individual who acts authoritatively with subordinates, but refuses to challenge outsiders. The president should be willing to joust with windmills, and he must be successful in tilting a few. He must be a champion for faculty welfare, student needs, and institutional freedoms and self-determination.

The president must care genuinely for the health and prosperity of the institution, and others must come to know that he cares. He must communicate continuously, informing and reminding others of common goals, thrusts, and efforts, as well as of successes or failures in progress. When demands are made upon others, these must be accompanied by a rational explanation. The president must be seen as acting in the best interests of all constituencies, or at least his intentions must be so accepted. He must be willing to provide an example of hard work and dedication, if he expects these characteristics to be exhibited by others within the college.

The president must not appear to be self-aggrandizing. He must not appear to be a social climber in the community or the state, or to have ambitions beyond his present position. He is wise not to become overly involved with the organizational politics of his professional group or mired in local civic affairs. These may assist in movement to other positions, but usually have little to do with the president's success in good institutional leadership internally.

The president must be genuinely interested in people. He must be willing to listen first, and he must be cautious in offering glib, superficial solutions for the problems of others. He must be a caring person. While he must be willing to take decisive action of a hurtful nature if circumstances demand, he must always be reluctant, and never callous, about doing so. He is sometimes the court of last resort for people with legitimate problems, and he must be an open and unbiased judge, as well as a merciful and just one.

The president must be cautious in his personal-social relationships, yet individuals within every college constituency must feel that they have a special relationship with him. These relationships must indeed be personal, yet not exclusionary. The president gives his time to people. Rather, he invests his time in people. The concept of invested time is significant, since it places a subtle obligation upon the recipient.

Surely it may be said that some of these approaches might not be effective in a larger campus situation. And certain of these may be irrelevant for the president who intends to spend only the norm of five years and move on, leaving accumulated and cancerous problems to another. However, most of these principles will be found to be effective for the president who wants to lead as if he intends to spend his career developing and enhancing a single institution and its quality of services.

THE PRESIDENT AS CHANGE-AGENT

The president must alternately assume the role of stabilizer and that of change-initiator in the college environment.

He must be a respecter of academic traditions and academic values characteristic of a collegiate institution. He must be steeped in faculty traditions. Since most traditions have their roots in academic bedrock, there is a rationale for their existence which may be enduring. The president should be extremely cautious in allowing departures from basic traditions except when these have been fully explored and the consequences examined. He should, in this case, be a stabilizing or restraining influence. Otherwise the institution would embark upon tangential errors or become a maverick within the peer community of like institutions, the latter often bearing a questionable reputation of low standards.

As stabilizer, the president restrains positive change which could come so rapidly as to cause turbulence, uncertainty, and anxiety among constituent groups. In this case it is the pace of change, and not its direction, which receives the president's attention. He must exert this restraint, even though some will never believe his protestations that he favors the movement—but at a more deliberate rate, and the negative camp will consider him as too easy.

While stability is necessary to the peace, order, and calm necessary for the teaching and learning process, change is necessary for progress and even for survival. If the institution is to adapt to a changing service climate, then the president must be willing to accept and to initiate change. The internal structure and dynamics for the institution should be such that change proposals of merit percolate to the top from all levels. There must be an atmosphere which encourages initiative, even though a screening process must also be functioning. An idea is not necessarily a good one just because it starts in a faculty or student committee. But neither is it a bad one because it begins with a group of secretaries or a security officer.

The president is duty bound to espouse, and to place in effect where his authority allows, those good ideas which emerge. He is not duty bound to the bad ones. Since he must assume the responsibility, he must be the judge of good and bad.

However, the president must often initiate change himself. Ordinarily, the best route is to place an idea into the institutional mill and let it make its way back with amplifications and some new twists. Although the president may know exactly what his position is within an area he is proposing for study, it may be best to put the matter up for discussion with appropriate advisory groups in which the initiative remains with his office, but a sounding given and different viewpoints articulated. Often an open-minded president will find his opinions changing while listening to the different points of view expressed.

Implied in all the above is a sensitivity to needed change on the part of the president. While others may be in positions of greater sensitivity to the need for change in administrative and procedural minutiae, the president himself is in the most advantageous position to sense the need for significant change, new thrusts, or broad institutional adaptation. The president discerns the need for change, i.e. he senses or discovers the need. Although frequently the need simply presents itself in clearly recognizable form, or comes as the result of purposeful research and study, the process of discernment must not be discounted. The process of discernment involves listening, reading, observing, and sensing, all leading toward thoughtful consideration and response on the part of the president and his advisors.

It goes without saying that changes are guided by the overarching vision that the president has for the institution. This clear and frequently articulated vision forms a general configuration within which specific changes are initiated or accepted. Those which are not compatible with the vision are rejected, and those which will lead toward the vision are accepted and supported.

MOTIVATION

Then outspake brave Horatius,
The Captain of the Gate:
"To every man upon this earth
Death cometh soon or late.
And how can man die better
Than facing fearful odds,
For the ashes of his fathers,
And the temples of his gods."
(Thomas B. Macaulay: "Horatius," *Lays of Ancient Rome*)

While seldom do those in public service positions face life or death situations, the president whose primary motivation is not altruistic will not find a high level of job satisfaction in his service. Although the presidency is more financially rewarding than other positions within the profession, it ranks well below most positions of a similar level in private business. Although there remains considerable status and public recognition associated with the position, these attributes have been countered by vulnerability to public criticism and unfavorable media attention when issues arise. The power base of the presidency is no longer sufficiently strong to satisfy those with such ambitions.

The president must have genuine social service motivation in order to find comfort in his position. He must believe in education as a necessary process for fruition in careers and attainment of a suitable quality of life. He must see himself and the institution as making contributions to society itself, as well as providing needed opportunities for the individuals it serves. He must enjoy the comradeship of other educational professionals in a common crusade of great and lasting worth.

Finally, the president must not depend upon the accolades received from others in judging his own merit, or his professional and personal worth. Praise is fleeting, and appreciation and gratitude are transient at best. In fact, the president will find himself in periods of personal stress when it appears that no one really cares about his contributions and sacrifices, nor even about the welfare of the college and its future. It is best if he is able to accept accolades when these are received, enjoy them for the moment, but not take them too seriously. It should come as no surprise that others will forget his triumphs and successes. Laurel wreaths wilt and badges of honor rust.

In the final analysis, the president's satisfactions and rewards are internal. Only the president knows and understands the real accomplishments which have been made and the difficulties which have been overcome. Only the president will understand the ambitions he has had for the college, and the pleasures and the disappointments he has experienced. He must accept the changes and vicissitudes of fortune philosophically, becoming neither enamored with his successes nor despondent about his setbacks. In the end, he is the only one who is able to make valid judgments about his performance and its merits.

One should not leave the subject of personal motivation in the presidency without some mention of the negatives, the downside of the motivational equation. The loneliness surrounding the occupant of the presidency may be overwhelming at times. Since all close friendships carry with them both a personal and a professional vulnerability, the president cannot afford close friendships among those with whom he has the most in common. He comes to understand that there are few, if indeed any at all, situations in which he is separated from his position. He comes to know that no one has a perspective from which to understand his problems, much less his personal feelings. While some may share his jubilation about successes which bode well for the college, few understand the depths of his disappointments over failures. Few can understand the president's role as victim, or scapegoat, when all does not function well within the college, or a well publicized failure occurs in the institutional systems of control.

In addition to the loneliness of the position, there are negatives for the president's family which cause some stress on the president as a conscientious spouse and parent. Growing up in the president's home on campus is not easy for children. Growing up as the son or daughter of a leading public figure in the community is not an easy task. Children of a president may at times be accorded privileges which most others do not have. However, they frequently encounter frustrations, and even hostilities, which others feel toward the college, its governance, or the president for perceived effronteries. Unfortunately, some may find it safer to attack, misuse, or abuse the president's family when opportunity presents itself, than to make a more frontal assault on the president or the institution itself.

The fishbowl effect itself often produces some adjustment and adaptation problems for the president and his family. While the spouse may understand the necessity of the family's life being subject to scrutiny by both college people and the general public, this is not always easy for children to understand. Sons and daughters of ministers, physicians, psychologists, government leaders, and others have some similar problems in accepting admonitions that they should somehow be different and above reproach because of their parent's role and position. It is difficult for a child or an adolescent to be perfect.

The role of the president's spouse is a difficult one. This has long been recognized for wives, but the role of the president's husband may present new, and perhaps more complex, challenges. This is sometimes seen by boards to be similar to that of *consort*, yet in most instances it is better that the husband be accepted as having a career of his own, independent of the wife and the college. Appearing in a supportive role to his spouse is viewed quite positively as a rule, however.

While almost every president resolves to reserve time for his family, few are able to do this as planned. Also, it appears from some observations that the president who is most careful to reserve time for professional reading, personal writing, fitness and exercise, spiritual concerns and religious activities; time for attendance at professional meetings, personal recreation, and spouse and children, is likely to be an ineffective and short-term president. Such a compunctious president simply has too many reservations to give of himself as the position requires.

Although the president may be fortunate enough to have a very accepting and understanding family, he must at times remind himself of personal priorities. It is well also that the president understands that when all the chips are down and everything has fallen apart at the college, his family may well be the only bona fide supporters left at his side.

Topics for Discussion or Further Study

1. In three or four sentences, give a summary definition of the aura of the presidency.

2. What conflicts may be inherent in the exercise of both power and compassion? Give examples.

3. Arrange a hierarchy of presidential allegiances and provide a rationale.

4. Is there a place for exercise of authority in the leadership of today's colleges? Under what conditions?

5. What are the "managerial" aspects of the presidency, as differing from the "leadership" facets?

6. What are some of the systems of classification for leadership or management styles according to other authors?

7. Develop two case study situations: one in which the president must act as change agent and one in which the president must be a stabilizer.

8. Why is the presidency often referred to as a lonely position?

PREPARATION FOR THE PRESIDENCY

2

Regardless of the increasing pressures and complications of the presidency, each time there is an opening search committees are inundated with applicants. Why? Has ambition overcome rationality within the profession? Does the system of administrative development produce a bounty of well prepared professionals ready to move into the top leadership position? Is there a lack of understanding of what the duties of the presidency really entail? Is there a void of understanding of the personal commitment and the toll which the presidency takes on both the individual and his/her family? Are the rewards and benefits of other positions, compared with those of the presidency, too small?

Perhaps the best answer to these and similar questions is a qualified affirmative. From experience in examining the credentials of candidates for the presidency, as well as for other administrative positions, it is clear that some aspire beyond their level of experience and qualifications. Some are evidently enamored with the status of the position, giving little thought to the actual conduct of the office. Further, one who has not been a president will never understand fully the broad scope of its duties or the demands which it makes upon the occupant and those near and dear. Leadership intern programs sometimes foster premature ambition among trainees, as do university graduate degree programs in community college administration. There are always those within the institution or the junior college sector anxious to test the Peter Principle, with great assurance that it is not applicable in their case.

Nevertheless, within almost every applicant pool there are from five to ten persons who appear to have appropriate credentials and experience to become worthy and viable candidates for presidential openings. Normally, these come from the ranks of less rewarding presidencies or from those in upper echelon positions. The system does indeed produce persons who are prepared to assume greater responsibility, and who show evidence of the potential to execute successfully these added duties. Some will later prove themselves.

THE PROPER BACKGROUND

Numerous treatises have appeared discussing the ideal background for the community or junior college presidency. Further, several good research studies have been made of the backgrounds of current community college presidents and of the opinions of community college presidents and others of the proper background for one seeking a presidency. The reader is referred to these for an empirical look at this important topic. George B. Vaughan has done outstanding work in this area. The discussion which follows represents the views of this author, which may be similar to many in the field but not necessarily congruent.

Some writers suggest that the expectations of the presidency call for an individual with an unrealistic breadth and depth of experience and training. So it is frequently with the lists of desired personal characteristics, which no human could possibly meet. On occasion, descriptions in advertisements and recruitment materials for presidential vacancies have a very ambitious, if not unrealistic, portrayal of the person sought.

A quarter-century ago, when this writer moved from a full professorship and partial administrative assignment in a graduate university to become a junior college president, this was most unusual. It would still be considered unusual. At that time a preponderance of community college presidents were emerging from the public school systems as local institutions were similarly emerging. Today, most new presidents come from the ranks of upper echelon administrators, particularly those in instructional vice president or dean positions. In the view of this writer, this is a highly appropriate pattern.

The two-year college tier within higher education is a specialty all its own. While certainly there are similarities between and among tiers at the collegiate level, there are marked differences in philosophy, curriculum, student clientele, governance, and finance. Personnel relations are different, simpler in some ways and more complex in others. There is a different perspective on some of the major problems such as matriculation and transfer, admissions, remediation, counseling, instructional approach, and the other facets of operation.

However, all this is not to say that successful presidents may not come from varied backgrounds. Some can indeed make the transition from the university to the junior college, learn those things necessary, and these bring a needed increment of academic tradition which prevents drift away from the continent of academia.

Similarly, an academically-oriented and scholarly, public school administrator may find his way into college administration, sometimes at the presidential level, and be successful. Ordinarily, it is best if the entry is made at a lower level and advancement earned. While faculty may be accepting of a person from the university sector because of academic credentials, they are less accepting of their titular leader coming from a lower tier of education. Typically, these moves are viewed as political or as serving public relations. The public school administrator usually has more to learn, and more difficulty in adapting, than a person moving from within the collegiate world, even though he may begin ahead in such areas as finance and facilities.

As alluded to earlier, the ideal president should have credentials with a terminal degree and experience as a faculty person, preferably in a junior college. This ideal president should have experience as an academic administrator, a student personnel administrator and counselor, journalistic and/or public relations training, and a background in accounting and business management. It would help if the person also had architectural education and experience. And this, unfortunately, is only a partial listing.

Quite obviously few, if any, candidates for presidential positions have such an impressive array of qualifications. As a result, a number of searchers look only to those experienced presidents in other institutions who want to move. This is a grievous error. While indeed a person with past experience as a president has some modicum of background in these various areas, these candidates may carry baggage which could be a handicap in the new situation. Certainly, this should not be the exclusive group explored.

Having spent twenty-five years at the helm of the same institution, this writer admits to some prejudice. While there are indeed many good presidents looking for an assignment with greater potential or better fitting their individual preferences, there are also those who are running from a bad experience, at least partially of their own making. There are those who do not wear well locally, and who must look for another position every three or four years. Work habits, interpersonal relations, staff conflicts, personal habits and idiosyncrasies, failure of style, and numerous other problems may lie behind an impetus to move and tendencies to be transient.

Searchers would be wise to be wary of those with long and impressive resumes, not only in different positions but in their listings of offices held in professional organizations, papers presented in meetings, innovative programs, and the like. Again, this is not meant to say that these may not be indicators of professionalism. However, some with such impressive records may be "organizational politicians."

Most readers have known persons who, either in neglect of their own enterprise or because of performance problems, look toward having their names on meeting programs or holding office in associations as a principal means of proving themselves worthy and satisfying ego needs which are unmet in job success. Some, who are undistinguished in other ways, may latch on to some new or unusual program thrust in an effort to obtain notice. While this syndrome may be atypical, searchers should have an awareness of it.

All this would appear to be downgrading to colleague presidents who may want to make a professional move. This is not the intent. Rather it is a lengthy discussion of reasons why all new presidents with potential may not come from these ranks. This author hastens to add that the best single source of persons to fill a presidential vacancy satisfactorily and with some predictable level of quality in performance would indeed be individuals with successful experience as presidents at other institutions.

Following the lateral move of another successful president, the next single best source for a new president should be from the ranks of top academic administrators, whether this be titled dean or academic vice president. Experience as a general or academic vice president exposes an individual to many of the same internal issues and problems with which the president must deal. As an aside, it should be noted that some institutions are quite liberal with grandiose titles for performance of limited functions. Searchers must be cautious about being overly impressed by titles alone.

As a president, the academic administrator will have to learn more about dealing with the external constituencies. He will also have to learn different facets of the same internal areas with which he has dealt previously. Budgeting must be learned from the source and the auditing and accounting views, for instance. Facilities planning and development must be learned from the design, materials, and business views. Nevertheless, some five years or more as an academic administrator tends to be the best background for a person desiring to move to the presidential level and perform successfully.

Much has been said and written about the administrative internship as a professional development experience. This writer looks positively upon such experiences, but would not recommend the employment of an individual solely on this basis. If an intern coming from the instructional ranks plans to move directly into a presidency, disappointment is both likely and appropriate. If an individual goes into an internship from the dean or vice president ranks, he may be an appropriate candidate. Much depends upon the success and satisfactoriness of the previous administrative experience. The internship experience is probably much less significant than is the quality of the person who undergoes the experience.

Similar comments may be made about doctoral programs in community college administration or higher education administration. A new doctoral person with little actual background in college administration is a poor candidate for a presidency, but may be a good candidate for a second or third echelon administrative position with opportunity to advance. Other things being equal, an individual coming from administrative ranks with a doctorate in higher education administration should be a better candidate for president than one with a doctorate in an academic discipline.

This writer has considerable respect for graduate training in collegiate administration. However, a brief critique may be in order. Too often such training is highly theoretical. Sometimes research techniques may be overly stressed in their minutiae, rather than in their practicality and applications. Some functions such as planning, accreditation, facilities, student personnel, personnel administration, and business management may be slighted. Too often, university program faculty have little or no background in actual administration of a college. Nevertheless, products of these programs have some advantage in perspective over those who have never had exposure to such academic education.

In summary, it appears that the most appropriate background for entering the presidency would be experience as a principal academic administrator with a doctorate in higher education administration. However, much depends upon the individual and his own peculiar characteristics and set of experiences. Certainly, at times the best choice may be a student personnel administrator or possibly even a business officer or institutional planner. Academic administrators, nevertheless, tend to be more readily accepted by the most significant internal constituency group, the faculty.

The writer recalls serving for a decade as a director and chairman of the board of a relatively large insurance corporation. The president and C.E.O. of the company decided that it would be best if the principal vice presidents were rotated in office each three years. Thus, the vice president for marketing would become the vice president for finance, the vice president for finance would become the head of claims processing, and the claims processing person would move to marketing, etc. The results were interesting. Every three years there was a period of some disruption due to change, and each had to learn things about the new position that the leaver already knew. As a cross-training experiment with potential for discovery of the best new chief executive officer possibility, it was a success. But for smoothness and efficiency, as well as progress, the procedure failed as square pegs and round holes appeared.

This serves to illustrate that there may be very few of those in principal administrative offices who could serve equally well in other positions in our institutions. If such there be, go mark him well, for he is presidential timber. But it is foolish to suggest that experience in all the principal offices should be a prerequisite to the presidency, or that rotational cross-training is a desirable practice in higher education.

MENTORING

Perhaps special mention of one of the more recently publicized techniques of administrative development is appropriate to any discussion of presidential aspirants. The reference to "more recently publicized" in language rather than a term such as "new technique" is an effort to be accurate. There is nothing new about mentoring. It has only recently been recognized and given respectability as a proper procedure, due open note and credibility. Once this might have been considered an instrumentality of the "good old boy" network. But since it has been recognized as a way to bring under-represented groups into the mainstream of college or business administration, it has emerged from the closet with a flourish.

Although it is subject to misuse and abuse, this approach has great potential for inducting new persons into administration and into the presidency itself. It is, in a sense, a special type of internship. Both the mentor and the internee have selected one another, forming a unique personal and professional relationship.

Others have written on the pitfalls, as well as the values, of the mentor relationship. These need not all be recited here. Suffice it to say that the relationship must indeed be a professional one. Further, either an open or a less formal mentor relationship may evoke jealousies and other in-house reactions which hamper other functions. This is, of course, less likely to occur when the trainee is already one of the chief subordinates to the president.

Through the years, many presidents have recognized talent and potential among staff and have arranged special experiences to develop the talent and promotions as growth has occurred. In a sense, these were mentor relationships, though never formally recognized as such, and these have a place in the profession. The president may take time to visit at length with select persons with potential, to advise and to encourage them, and to discuss professional issues. He may also arrange for attendance at seminars and meetings beyond those normally made available. While there is some risk in doing so, he counts this as time and money invested in the future of that individual and in improvement of the profession.

Before leaving this topic, it is well to note that this technique, whether formal or informal, is indeed one of the better procedures for bringing women and minorities into the upper echelons of administration. Careful nurturance and special opportunities for professional development may be highly significant in making collegiate administration, and the presidency in particular, an equal opportunity profession.

ASPIRANTS AND VACANCIES

The purpose of this section is to offer advice to presidential aspirants, as is perhaps the overriding purpose of the entire book. All advice received by an individual who aspires to become a president should be evaluated and sifted. Certainly that admonition includes that which is offered here. Just as there is no single route toward the presidency, there is no set formula to follow in seeking that position.

It is well for an aspirant to do a great deal of self-evaluation. He should look at his own characteristics and background in a critical way. He should compare himself with others who hold or are seeking a presidency. He should be sure that his ambitions are not premature, i.e. in terms of maturity, credentials, and experience. He should consider the sacrifices, as well as the rewards, which go with movement into the presidential ranks. As a president, he will never live anything approaching a normal life again.

While youthfulness may indeed have many advantages in life, one of these is not normally impressiveness as a presidential candidate. Most successful contenders are beyond the age of forty, although a few have achieved the office a few years earlier. Few successful presidential contenders, without past experience in the position, are over the age of fifty-five. The prime period for attaining the first presidency tends to be around the forty-five to fifty age range. Boards tend to look at youthful candidates as more vigorous, but more prone to mistakes in judgment. They look at older candidates as more stable and less controversial, but less vigorous and active.

Thus, it would appear that the best advice for a youthful candidate would be to emphasize his maturity and stability, while dressing his vigor and change-agent tendencies in gowns of rationality. The older candidate might well stress his youthful idealism and vitality, while letting his experience and mature perspective be shown as dynamic in nature.

Much depends, of course, on what qualities the searchers are wanting in their president. Candidates should be aware that neither the published material nor the orally expressed characteristics may be fully indicative of those which will actually guide the selection. A search group that has announced its desire for a mature and experienced president may be most impressed by the youthful enthusiasm of a candidate who does not meet the description. This is to say that there may be an unwritten set of characteristics of which even the searchers are consciously unaware, and/or that searchers are sometimes impressionable people who may be influenced spontaneously.

Candidates should also be aware that not all vacancies are real. Because of legal prescriptions, vacancies are sometimes advertised when the selection has in all practicality been made. When such is the case, the candidate can expect no one connected with the search to say that it is not an open one, and it is offensive to ask. Sometimes others with inside knowledge may suggest that some person has an "inside track." If the candidate obtains such information from a friendly and reliable (although unofficial) source, it is better to avoid the race.

However, it has been the experience of this writer that more presidential searches are truly open than some critics believe. Even in those cases where an inside candidate has been selected in the final outcome, searchers have been honestly measuring the other candidates against this person as a standard. The familiarity of the inside candidate as a known entity gives that person some advantage if the comparison is close. Most board members, and to a lesser degree most faculty, tend to make a real effort to be objective in evaluating candidates, although faculty have a personal stake in the outcome.

When the predominant influence in the selection process comes from the faculty and staff sectors, the tendency will be toward the candidate who has leadership qualities but is less threatening. This is not an indictment of the integrity of searchers or committee members from the employee sector. It is just a simple statement of the self-protective psychology that is quite natural to persons in these positions. Often, this mental and emotional process leads these groups to favor some known internal candidate who may not have exemplified the strength which is needed in a president, or faculty may be dubious of a strong, assertive colleague who may be good administrative timber. Board members need to be aware of such tendencies.

Also, there appears to be some cycling, or pendulum effect, in that if the last president has been a strong, dominant leader with authoritative characteristics, faculty searchers will tend to look favorably at candidates who profess and demonstrate different qualities. It must also be understood that the opposite will tend to occur. If the last president has been weak and indecisive, and something akin to anarchy characterizes internal affairs, both board and faculty searchers will tend to prefer a candidate who impresses them as strong and assertive, a "take charge" type.

The resume' may well be the most significant of all considerations in the emergence of presidential hopefuls from the general field into a select group of contenders. For this reason, its careful preparation is of great importance. Moderation is suggested in terms of length and detail. A resume' which only sketches briefly in one page the educational and work history of the candidate is insufficient. Likewise, one which is ten or twenty pages and details every committee assignment, every paper presented, and every movement or event with which the candidate has ever been associated, is too much.

The resume' should give in some detail the work history, personal background, and educational background of the candidate. It is beneficial as well that it present the candidate's major accomplishments as an administrator and major professional contributions. Leadership roles of a non-educational nature are significant also. But the candidate must not inundate the searchers with material.

Personal contacts with searchers should be made with great caution. It is well for the candidate to telephone the head of the search group to ascertain if his material has been received and to express his sincere interest in the position. Personal contact with individual members of the search group, unless they are acquaintances, is not recommended.

If the candidate has friends who are acquaintances of search group members, a few contacts on his behalf may be of assistance, but only a few. Also, if he has friends who are presidents, board members, or professionals, and who have positive knowledge of his competencies, a couple of letters which suggest that he is a good prospect may be helpful. This tends to be true even if the search procedures do not call for recommendations at this stage.

Such limited contacts will tend to attract enough attention from searchers that it will help the candidate move from the applicant pool to the list of serious contenders. It must be noted, however, that these must appear to be casual "nominations" rather than an orchestrated campaign, and this effort should not be over done.

Choice of references is of great importance. There is a tendency to name the most important personages within one's sphere of acquaintance as references, and this is not all bad. However, some attention should be given to the constituencies represented on the search group, when these are known to the candidate. If there are faculty on the group, then references from faculty leaders draw attention. Board references draw attention from that constituency. References from presidents are normally good, particularly presidents under whom the person has served. The candidate should strive for a balance in the references presented.

While some search groups will request that reference letters be submitted with materials, as a rule references become most important when the selection process has reached its final stages. The candidate should, of course, alert references that they may be contacted. Often, such contacts are made by telephone, as searchers have become aware that they are more likely to receive candid answers to questions and candid opinions over the telephone than in writing.

There may be little in the way of worthwhile advice to offer candidates regarding the interview process for finalists. The candidate must convey a genuine interest in the position, and be prepared to state convincingly his reasons for desiring it. Conversely, he must not appear desperate or overly eager. He needs to demonstrate confidence and poise, without appearing egotistical. He must be prepared to present himself and his work positively, without appearing to be bragging.

While being consistent in his statements of administrative philosophy, the candidate must try to avoid offending any of the constituencies present. This is not to say, however, that the candidate should not be honest and forthright in a diplomatic fashion. A "wishy-washy" candidate will lose on all fronts. The candidate must not pretend to be something which he is not. While sometimes pretensions may help to land the position, these will soon be found out after arrival on the scene.

Candidates should be prepared to answer questions and to explain views on a number of different subjects, particularly any issues which are "hot" at that time within the institution or within educational circles in general. Invariably questions will be raised on matters such as administrative approach or philosophy. Sometimes hypothetical situations (which may or may not be hypothetical) will be posed. Usually, the general background of a viable candidate provides enough perspective to enable extemporaneous responses of substance to most questions asked. On occasion, but not too often, the candidate may have to answer that some time and study is necessary prior to taking a position on the issue.

Oftentimes candidates are extended a number of special courtesies in connection with an institutional visit and interview. It is well to write notes of appreciation to persons who have been helpful. The candidate should also follow up with a letter to the search group expressing appreciation for courtesies and consideration, and reiterating interest in the institution and the position.

Perhaps a word to those aspirants who are unsuccessful as candidates may be appropriate. Since there are normally several well-qualified candidates for any position, an unsuccessful one should certainly not be discouraged from seeking other presidencies which may open. It is useful to examine one's experience in the current contest, and to learn from it. Sometimes this can best be done in consultation with a mentor or other professional friend, sharing in detail that which transpired. Those characteristics which did not impress one search group may impress the next, but some adjustments in approach may need to be made.

It is prudent for the candidate to convey the impression of a good loser to the search group and others at the institution where he was unsuccessful. Sometimes there are positive impressions made which may transfer via the informal network to another college where a vacancy occurs. Several observers, including this writer, have seen this actually happen.

It is also important that sensitive efforts be made in educational and administrative development programs to provide opportunities for obtaining the necessary experience, professional growth, credentials, and mentoring to enable candidates from under-represented groups to compete successfully in presidential searches.

Topics for Discussion or Further Study

1. What do research surveys reported in the literature show regarding the backgrounds of currently serving presidents? Be reasonably specific and give citations.

2. Develop an argument for each of the following positions as preparing for the presidency: chief business officer; chief student personnel officer; institutional research director; personnel officer.

3. Should actual administrative experience of some type, or graduation from a graduate program in higher education administration, be prerequisites to entry? Give both the positives and negatives of such a requirement.

4. Should an internship or mentoring experience be required for graduation from a graduate program in higher education administration? Give both positives and negatives of such a requirement.

5. Prepare a resume' which might be submitted by you as an appli-
    cant for the presidency of a two-year college with 1,500 full-time
    equivalent students located in a community of 5,000 population in
    the Midwest heartland. Feel free to enhance your qualifications
    with fictitious experiences as appropriate, keeping in mind reali-
    ties of the process and what has been learned. (Note: The resume'
    might be considered as a rough blueprint for development as a
    bona fide presidential applicant.)

7. As a class activity, conduct a group activity screening the resumes
    presented by class members and providing critiques for guidance.

8. Conduct mock interviews for a fictitious presidency, such as that
    described, with class members role-playing different representa-
    tional constituencies on the selection committee.

PRESIDENTIAL SEARCHES

3

The purpose of this chapter is to provide a general framework guiding the search process and the procedures in carrying through with the process. While it is not intended as a "cookbook" presentation, it may provide information helpful in planning the conduct of a search which has promise of meeting the needs of an institution with a presidential vacancy.

CONSULTANTS

One of the first decisions to be made by the governing board is whether to employ a consultant or a consulting organization to assist in planning and conducting the search procedure. There are both advantages and disadvantages to doing so.

Much depends upon the relationship of the board with the outgoing president. If the board has confidence in this president, and if he has the time, the competencies, and the willingness to assist and guide them through the entire process, then he may well serve as their consultant. It is helpful if the president also has the general confidence of the faculty. He must not be seen as manipulating the process in any way, or as trying to fulfill his own agenda in naming a new president of his choice.

If the outgoing president is to fill the role of consultant, then it must be made clear to all internal constituencies, external groups, and candidates when appropriate, that he is in the role of consultant to the board, and that the role of consultant does not include active participation in the selection decision. The outgoing president should also make it clear to the board and to others that he does not seek or desire to name his successor, and that he would consider it inappropriate to be actively involved in the decision itself. While he has a right to his opinions, the same as others do, he must be cautious in expressing these except on request of board or search group members.

The president's office staff may perform the clerical duties necessary to the conduct of the search. It is very important that office staff treat all materials, correspondence, discussions, and records with great confidence during the entire search process. Human characteristics being as they are, others will be pumping office staff for information which they cannot receive through official channels. Records should, of course, be kept secure.

The question arises as to what consultants and consulting services may do to assist the process. The first thing which comes to mind is that they may assure that the process is kept legal throughout. This is extremely important. The search procedure must follow legal prescriptions and guidelines. There must be a genuine effort to secure an applicant pool which is broad and unselected. To put it another way, the search process must provide equal opportunity for all qualified applicants to become a part of the pool. Throughout the deliberations no hint of any form of prejudice can be tolerated. Evaluative criteria must not reflect any preconceived bias.

A consultant will assist the board in developing and defining its search mechanics. If an advisory group or a search committee is to be set up, the consultant may help in defining the constituency of that group and its responsibilities. After visiting with the board, and its search group, the consultant may define the characteristics which the institution hopes to find in a new president, assist in developing evaluative criteria for candidates, prepare publicity and advertisements for circulation, and carry out other delegated duties. He may give guidance on screening the pool and procedures for selection of candidates for more intense consideration. He may make suggestions regarding procedures for choosing finalists, contacting references, and for the logistics of interviewing.

One of the decisions which the board and its search team must make is whether to allow the consultant organization to screen applicants and present to them a smaller number of contenders. Most presidential searches may draw from thirty to one hundred applicants. The process of studying materials submitted may be a laborious one. This task may be delegated to a consultant organization.

However, this writer strongly recommends that the consultant or consultant organization not be delegated the task of screening, and that this be performed by the search team itself. It is extremely important that candidates who may interest local persons not be screened out by professionals acting in their behalf. Screening of candidates gives a healthy sense of participation to those constituencies involved in the search.

Also, it must be understood that search consultants and consultant organizations sometimes have an agenda of their own. Consultants may have professional and personal ties and acquaintances which may predispose their judgments. There is always the danger of something akin to the "good old boy network" which can come into play, although in this case it may tend to be more one of organizational politics. Some consultant firms double as "head hunters" and placement bureaus, and this may pose conflicts of interest.

For these reasons, the writer recommends the use of a single consultant, rather than a consulting service. If the local milieu and other relationships are right, the outgoing president may serve in this role. If there is any doubt, however, a single outside consultant most certainly is preferred.

As a means of controlling expenses, it is suggested that a consultant be identified within the state or region in which the college is located. Although it is frequently denied and is often considered with a negative connotation, the truth is that there is a certain degree of provincialism present in most institutional situations. A consultant from the general geographic area is likely to have a much better understanding of the local milieu and the cultural, as well as educational, considerations relevant to it.

It should be noted that some boards may have sufficient expertise to conduct proper presidential searches without the benefit of professional staff assistance or consultative help. However, this is not the norm. Most boards would be wise to seek assistance of knowledgeable professionals to guide them through the process.

THE RECRUITMENT PROCEDURE

It would be beneficial for boards to consider the search process as one of recruitment and promotion, as well as one of selection. This suggests, of course, an organized publicity campaign.

Advertisement comes quickly to mind as a major technique in recruitment, and properly so. The placement of advertisements in one or more of the major professional news media is a must. Not only will this reach the widest professional audience, but also it will tend to broaden the pool of applicants in keeping with proper equal opportunity efforts.

In the case of community and junior college vacancies, perhaps the best communication may be made through those newspapers which are focused on this particular sector. This is not to suggest that a broader higher education medium may not be employed, but that the others provide a more focused effort at less cost. The size of the advertisement is not as significant as its presence. Advertisements should run at least three weeks, preferably a little longer. Advertisements need provide only the basic information about the vacancy, giving the reader an address and/or telephone number to call for more information.

Direct mail contacts are important. The institution should send out printed materials describing the position, citing the general qualifications needed, giving a brief description of the institution and its setting, providing information on the manner in which applications are to be prepared, and the process for receiving applications. It is important that this flyer be carefully prepared, and that it be brief but informative.

This printed material should be broadly circulated. If cost is not a factor, it should be sent to administrators in every two-year college in the country. If choices must be made, then those in the geographic region may be targeted. Departments of higher education in graduate universities, as well as placement offices, are also important targets.

It should be emphasized that the direct mail campaign should seek nominations as well as applications. Current presidents and other professionals are rich sources of information in the identification of candidates who may not be actively seeking a new position, and thus not reading advertisements.

While not denigrating the value of advertising, it must be said that broad advertisement tends to yield a number of applicants who may not be the best available. Although some quality candidates are watching advertisements for an opportunity of a professional upgrade, so also are those who find themselves under pressures in their current positions. For these reasons, the direct mail and nomination efforts are extremely significant.

There should be a procedure in place, of course, for responding to nominations with a letter and mailing of printed materials, just as there should be a response letter to all applicants who submit their personal materials.

The printed material and the advertisements should tell potential applicants what is to be sent as an application. While some institutions prefer a structured application, others simply ask for a resume' with only a few specifics mentioned, such as names, addresses, and telephone numbers of references. Some ask for a brief biography, and others ask for some written statement on educational philosophy. The writer suggests that only the minimum specifics be provided in structure, leaving applicants free to format their resumes as they wish. It is suggested also that formal letters of recommendation not be solicited with the application.

Printed recruitment material should inform applicants concerning the deadline for submittal of applications. It should also inform them of any other dates in a planned timetable for selection while leaving some impression of flexibility in these.

Applicants have a right to be informed concerning the confidentiality of their application and of the material which they submit. It goes without saying that these statements regarding confidentiality must be respected by everyone involved. If there is a point at which confidentiality can no longer be kept, due to sunshine laws or other reasons, the applicants should be informed of that fact. If this is to occur at a certain stage of the process, such as in the finalist stage, each applicant should be reminded of that as notice is issued regarding attainment of finalist status.

It should be said that there is no need for dragging out a search process interminably. Good candidates are lost when a search process stretches on and on. A well organized search and selection process can be started and concluded in a period of four months or less. A search period of six months or more is unnecessary. The quicker the search is concluded, providing it is a thorough one with proper procedures, the quicker the institution can begin to settle down from the distractions associated with these activities.

ORGANIZING THE SEARCH

It must be understood that no other decision is likely to be as important to as many people around the college as the selection of a new president. No other decision is likely to be as important to the future of the institution over the next few years as that choice. Everyone is interested, and there must be good communication of appropriate information to various constituencies throughout the process. At no point is clarity of communication more important than in the written and oral statements which describe the process to be followed.

This writer will reveal an early bias by stating forthrightly that the governing board must maintain control of the decision-making process in the selection of a new president. This is a legal obligation of the board, and it is their duty to follow it through. They must make it clear exactly what the participation of others will be, yet reserve the right of final decision. It is, of course, wise to involve others in the process.

Searches are organized in any number of different ways. Some involve large search committees made up of board members, faculty, support staff, students, and citizens. These tend to be terribly cumbersome, as would be the case with any large group regardless of composition. Sometimes an internal committee is given the task of screening applicants and furnishing the board with the names of only three to five finalists. This can be a delicate problem if none of the finalists are pleasing to the governing board, and if others are added (and eventually selected) outside the initial process.

Since it is imperative that the governing board not break faith with internal constituencies, then it follows that the search procedure must not only be clearly defined, but must also be one with which the board can be comfortable in its outcome. It is equally imperative that certain internal constituencies, in particular the faculty and administrators, be given a meaningful role in the search and selection process. A meaningful role may be advisory in nature rather than determinative. Even if the role is advisory, it must be one of genuine involvement and not a facade. The role must be clearly defined and clearly communicated so that there will be no misunderstandings.

It is suggested that the search committee be kept small, preferably from five to seven members. Further, it is suggested that this committee have two board members, one of whom will serve as chairman. Possibly three board members might be included if it is a seven member group. There should be one member representative of the upper echelon administrators, and two or more members representative of the faculty (including department heads). If there is a titular head of a faculty organization, that individual should be one of the faculty representatives. Others may be chosen through an elective process, from certain ex-officio roles within the internal governance structure, or designated by the board.

Certain special cases are worthy of mention. In some instances there may be an administrator in the college with considerable merit and leadership ability. Unless this person is a candidate for the presidency, that administrator may be placed on the search committee. In such a case, it is permissible to ask the person directly whether or not candidacy is an intent. If there are internal candidates, and an appointive process is being used for certain choices free of ex-officio roles, then it is best to include neither known supporters nor known detractors of these candidates on the search committee. The purpose of this latter suggestion is to avoid the appearance of bias or of a "rigged" committee.

It will be noted that these suggestions do not include representation of students, support staff, or citizens. Citizen representation, members of the public, is assured by participation of the board itself. Students are extremely important, but they are transient consumers of institutional services and tend to lack the background, understanding, or long term interest to make a really helpful, positive contribution to the process. A better case might be made for the inclusion of one support staff member on the search committee. However, faculty, and related professionals such as librarians and counselors, and administrators are in the best position to render sound advice, and these are the most significant internal constituencies with whom the new president must work in order to achieve a successful leadership tenure. Some sacrifices must be made in order to keep the search group at a workable, interactive number.

The "charge" to the search committee must define its role and the entire process clearly. For instance, the board might, in a memo, tell the search committee the role of the consultant, if one is employed, prescribe the dates for submittal of evaluative criteria for board approval, indicate reporting dates or request a timetable for sanction, discuss confidentiality, delimit the committee's role, assign responsibility for material preparation and review, and state the reservations being withheld by the board for its own deliberation. A follow-up to the "charge" should be a briefing by the consultant, with the board chairman in attendance, covering these and other admonitions and directions orally.

The search committee should be required to report to the board regularly throughout the process. Two of these reportings have special significance. They are the submittal of the listings of semi-finalists and finalists. It is suggested that the semi-finalist list be one of eight or ten names. The finalist list may be only three to five names long.

If the board has reserved for all its members the right to review applications, whether or not this right is exercised, then it is appropriate for each member to have the privilege of adding one candidate to the list of semi-finalists. Similarly, the board as a whole might reserve the privilege of adding two to the list of finalists. Any such reservations should, of course, be spelled out in the "charge" memo, and should be clearly understood by all who are following the process. It is unlikely that these options will ever be exercised, but they may be safeguards in a process which needs careful planning and controls which may be exercised if required. The worst scenario is a significant alteration of a procedure after it has been announced, arranged, and has functioned. Minor adjustments may have to be made as unforeseen circumstances are encountered.

The logistics of the process need to be defined in some rudimentary fashion. If the applications are to be received in a certain office, this needs to be specified. If the search committee and its chairperson are to set up the logistics, then that assignment needs to be made.

The search committee should continue to be involved throughout the entire process, but its role tends to change once the finalists have been named. The board must make the final decision from among this group of finalists and, of course, must participate in the interviewing phase.

EVALUATIVE CRITERIA

Those qualifications which have been specified in the recruitment materials constitute evaluative criteria of a primary nature. However, these may (and should) be very limited. The recruitment material may specify that candidates must have an earned doctoral degree and administrative experience in higher education. These then become the first two criteria to be used in screening applicants. Those who do not meet these basic qualifications as stated should not be considered, of course. To do so, perhaps because of some personal or political pressure, not only undermines the entire process but also exposes the institution to legal vulnerability.

All of the criteria which may be developed into a listing may not be subject to evaluation and judgment based upon written submittals alone. Better judgments may be made after checking references, and even more information should be available after the interview stage. These things must be understood in the application of any set of listed criteria. Further, most criteria may not be met in total or at zero levels, but may instead be present in gradients. This suggests the need for some form of rating system, if candidates' merits are to be converted to numerical values. Finally, criteria are not of equal importance, so to be properly useful a numerical system of ratings would require some weighting of them.

For these reasons, most boards and search committees may find it more convenient and expedient to prepare listings of criteria and to perform ratings, but to screen or rank candidates based upon personal interactions and discussions of these rather than using a numerical system. Although numerical systems, if properly developed, will tend to yield similar results, these tend to be complex in design and cumbersome to use.

The criteria to be employed should be developed by the search committee, with the aid of the consultant. These should be submitted to the board for approval, then published internally within the college. No attempt will be made here to provide an exhaustive listing, and some of those mentioned below may not be appropriate for the listing of any specific institution. These are furnished simply as examples, and are not necessarily in any rank order of significance.

Exemplary criteria might include the following:

Holds an earned doctoral degree
Has substantive previous administrative experience
Has past experience in a two-year college
Has experience with both academic and technical education
Understands the cultural milieu of the college
Has experience with similar student clientele
Demonstrates the potential for assertive leadership
Has a participative approach to leadership
Demonstrates creativity and innovation
Appears to be stable in career pattern
Spouse is an asset
Appears to have charisma
Demonstrates a history of good working relations with:
    boards, students, faculty, public
Has good writing skills
Speaks well; has poise before groups
Understands institutional research and planning
Has experience with accreditation matters
Is scholarly in background and interests
Understands college finance, accounting, budgeting
Has experience with facilities planning and construction
Is familiar with professional issues
Demonstrates a time commitment to work load
Has a high energy and performance level
Demonstrates organizational abilities
Has strong ethical and moral reputation
Seems to possess good common sense
Active in community and civic affairs
Has general culture attributes appropriate to position

While the above list may not be exhaustive, and it may not stress certain attributes considered to be important to the local situation, it will serve as an example of the kinds of characteristics which might be sought in a new president, and thus the nature of the criteria upon which the applicant pool should be judged.

As indicated earlier, desired characteristics may be employed in the form of a checksheet by members of the search committee. It is best if each search committee member studies the applicant pool independently, completes his checklists and makes other notes, and then follows up with the actual screening which may occur in group sessions with each candidate receiving individual consideration. Logistics should provide for applicant pool material to be kept in an office under security and observation of an assigned person, but with opportunity and a place for search committee members to come and spend extensive time going through the material.

While it is not necessary or recommended that these individual reviews be done in a group setting, on occasion this may be the case. Neither is it necessary to wait until the application period is closed to begin review of materials. By the time the application period closes, a well organized search committee can have much of its study work done.

In the early processes, a rough screening in a group setting may be all that is necessary. When there is an agreement among search committee members that a given candidate's materials do not justify further consideration, these may be so classified without consuming additional time. Some committees tend to create three stacks: rejects; further consideration; and meritorious. Other titles may be used, of course, but certain candidates may be readily identifiable from previous intensive review of materials as unsuitable and others as promising.

Considerable attention should be directed toward the promising or meritorious group, and some additional attention should be given to the middle group to assure that no promising person has been overlooked. The promising group may tend to number some greater, but usually not too much greater, than the allowable number of semi-finalists. The task now is to identify the weaker members of the promising group, keeping in mind the criteria which have been previously adopted. If there are fifteen in the promising group and the allowable number of semi-finalists is ten, it is usually fairly easy to agree upon two or three to eliminate. After this, it may take considerable discussion to decide between and among another four to narrow the list. Perhaps it would be easier if it were understood that none of these have a high probability of becoming finalists. Nevertheless, all decisions at this stage should be taken seriously.

It should be mentioned again that the review and screening of candidates prior to the naming of some ten semi-finalists is done on the basis of paperwork submitted. This includes reference letters, if such have been requested or received, and nomination letters received. If there have been informal contacts relayed to the committee, these may be considered for whatever they may be worth. It is not appropriate for members of the committee, either individually or collectively, to be soliciting opinions or references prior to the semi-finalist stage. It is, however, wise for all to listen quietly to any information which passes within the purview of their senses.

Once the list of semi-finalists has been submitted to the board and approved, then it is time for the serious inquiries begin. Each candidate should be notified that he/she is a semi-finalist, and that reference checks will be made using the names submitted and possibly with other persons deemed to have knowledge of professional characteristics and functioning. Unless sunshine laws require the opening of the list of names to the media and for public scrutiny, the process should remain confidential until the finalist stage. This could mean that the semi-finalist list might be submitted to board members as information and, unless some action is desired, kept as informational. In either case, candidates must be informed of the change in confidentiality status and its limits.

It is best if all search committee members have identical exposure to official inquiries of references or of other persons with relevant knowledge. Telephone contacts will tend to result in more candid observations. It is suggested that these be made by the committee utilizing a speaker phone so that all may listen and make notes. The committee should, if reasonable, notify the references they have decided to call by mail, giving dates and approximate time periods for the intended calls.

It is understood, of course, that applicants will not list references from whom they would expect to receive anything other than a positive recommendation. For this reason, the contact list should not be confined to the recommendations furnished. Committee strategy may include certain sampling techniques, even though these tend to have certain, predictable biases. For instance, calling the president of the faculty association at an institution. Certain persons could be called by virtue of office such as the board chairman, the head of the department of mathematics, or the president of the chamber of commerce. These persons can be reached without being notified in advance. Sometimes, a member of the committee may have knowledge of other presidents or faculty within the vicinity who can furnish information or leads. This process of checking should be a thorough one, extensive in nature, and intensive in approach, but always done as a group or by specific delegation of the search group.

Prior to placing calls to references and knowledgeable persons, the committee should agree on a standard listing of questions to be asked. A structuring statement should be prepared so that each contact is given the same explanation. It should be decided in advance which committee member will take the lead, normally the chairperson, and who will ask certain questions. These conversations should be information gathering in nature, and it is not necessary or appropriate to be commenting prematurely on the process or its outcomes.

If there are ten semi-finalists, then three or four may be called into question as a result of committee contacts. It is well to stress again the need for evaluating the credibility and the bias of persons contacted. It is rare that a candidate should be ruled out on the basis of one, unsubstantiated, non-specific, bad reference. On the other hand, if a comment appears to conform to a pattern with the innuendos of others and with certain things in the written materials, then it must be taken seriously. Candidates may be "damned with faint praise," or condemned by glowing praise that becomes suspicious.

In an ideal situation, the committee would come to a consensus on the finalists as a result of open and intense discussion. Sometimes a "straw poll" by secret ballot will reveal that they are very close to agreement, but each may be trying to be very considerate and respectful of others. If so, this can be an aid to consensus. If all else fails, then a vote on those candidates who remain in contention is necessary. This should be an unweighted vote, with each member writing down the number of names allowable as finalists. If the allowable number emerges clearly, then the process is complete. If there are more than the allowable number who emerge clearly, but there's an obvious division on one or two slots, then a second vote should be taken among those contenders for the remaining slots.

Following the selection of the set number of finalists, normally three to five, most of the work of the search committee is completed. It may be, however, that during the interview procedure an audience with the search committee may be included. The search committee may then become an avenue for collection, evaluation, and interpretation of reactions and responses of various campus constituencies after interviews have been conducted with finalists. This is desirable, but it depends on the will of the governing board, which has the responsibility for the final selection.

INTERVIEWS AND THE DECISION

While the governing board must make the selection from among the finalists, it is good practice to allow various campus people to meet the candidates in both formal and informal settings. Meeting the candidates does not imply that a poll should be taken, or that there should be any formal solicitation of reactions. To do so would put the board and the new president at a disadvantage if the board should choose a candidate other than the poll winner. Neither should any memos signed by groups be considered, nor should any board member or search committee person conduct a poll of any nature. This does not mean, however, that search committee and board members do not have eyes to see what transpires or ears to hear what is being said.

The consultant, along with the search committee, may recommend interviewing procedures. These should involve a campus visit by each candidate and spouse for one day, perhaps a day and a half. The visits of candidates must be spaced so that these are not overlapping. During this period, both should meet informally with the search committee, perhaps for lunch or dinner, followed by a formal interview period. There should be opportunity for administrators and division heads to meet with the candidate. A representative group of faculty should meet for an hour or so with the candidate, along with a "coffee" for all to meet the candidate and spouse informally. The candidate should also meet with student government leaders, and an informal period may be arranged for the candidate and spouse to meet support staff members.

During the interview time, there should be opportunity for the entire board to meet both informally and formally with the candidate and spouse. Again, the informal period may be a luncheon or dinner while the formal period should be somewhat on the order of a structured interview. The board should prepare a list of questions to be asked of each candidate, but these should be asked in a way which does not appear to be stilted or formalistic. Each member may assume the responsibility for asking favored questions, with leading questions becoming the role of the chairman. Essentially, most questions will tend to be in the areas suggested by the criteria, in both the board and the search committee interviews.

It is important that each candidate be extended proper and similar courtesies, from first to last. This includes being furnished a schedule including the identification of some participants such as board members and search committee members by name. It should also include hotel reservations, expense payments, pick-up and escort services, and the like. Every candidate should be made to feel that they are a leading contender, which is true, and that their interest in the position is appreciated. Each should be treated as though they might be the new president.

Candidates should not be spared tough questions. However, it is important that proper professional courtesy prevail throughout. While the position of candidates may be solicited on issues of general importance within the institution, interviews should not degenerate to the airing of pet peeves or attempts to gain a pre-commitment on local issues with which candidates have no basis for familiarity. The search committee escort should intervene, if necessary, to keep this from happening, and to keep campus interview sessions from bogging down on single issue discussions. The board chairperson may exercise prerogatives in so directing those sessions.

After the campus interviews have been conducted, the question arises as how to proceed. Some boards and search committees may desire to schedule visits to the home campus of candidates. This is not recommended, and there are some precautions to take if it is done. First, this procedure should be used only if there are two top candidates and the decision between them is extremely difficult. Second, only a very small group should be involved in the visit, utilizing board members and search committee people. Third, the visit should be structured in advance. At best, such visits tend to be disrupting to the home campus, and very embarrassing to the losing candidate.

It is often difficult to ascertain the true circumstances on the home campus. If the candidate is unpopular there, he may be promoted by informal conspiracy for the new position. If the candidate is viewed as a strong and assertive person, as may be desired for the presidency, he may receive negative or qualified endorsements from certain campus people with whom he has had encounters. For these and the above reasons, campus visits are not suggested.

Returning to the point when interviews have been finished and the board faces a decision, it would be well for the entire board to meet one more time with the search committee. This is for the purpose of gleaning their views about each candidate and giving them opportunity to pass on to the board the things their constituents are saying. It should be said again that no committee member should be taking polls, but each should be expressing and interpreting what has been volunteered to him, and stating his own opinions identified as such. Likewise, the board should be taking no committee polls or votes, only listening and questioning committee members to ascertain their views. Normally, the procedure should involve taking one candidate at a time and discussing each, individually and in turn. When this is done the meeting should adjourn, without an effort by any board member to pass the responsibility for decision back to the committee.

When all relevant and proper input has been received and evaluated in executive session, then it is the prerogative of the board to meet in an official session and name the new president. Preferably, this should be a unanimous vote, even if there have been previous differences of opinion. Every new president deserves to start under conditions of unanimity.

A procedure such as the one above will tend to result in the selection of a suitable president, and perhaps even a good one. It should be noted that there is a difference in meaning between a suitable candidate and the best one, albeit a subtle distinction. Much depends upon the sensitivity and the intuitiveness of the board itself as to whether the institution gets the type of president it wants or the type it needs. These may be congruent, of course, but not necessarily. This nuance should receive deliberate attention in the process.

Topics for Discussion or Further Study

1. Utilizing role-playing techniques, conduct a mock session with class members playing the role of board members as they discuss procedures for a presidential search.

2. Develop a list of seven evaluative criteria in presidential selection which you believe to be the most important. Place these in order of priority. Provide a rationale.

3. Imagine yourself as a consultant to whom a search procedure has been given in written form for evaluation and critique. Make a list of points or criteria upon which you might evaluate the propriety and wisdom of this procedure.

4. From your knowledge and what is accessible in the literature, what are the most frequent errors made in conduct of presidential searches?

5. Why must the governing board be the final authority in the selection of a president?

6. Provide a rationale for regionalism as an influence in the selection of a president. Provide an argument against the influence of regionalism in such a decision.

7. What steps may be taken to assure that the selection process truly provides equal opportunity for candidates from groups underrepresented in the presidency?

TRANSITIONS

4

Although transition in leadership constitutes the most abrupt and noticeable of all transitions an institution may undergo, it is not the only form of transition that can significantly affect its future. However, a transition in the presidency may well be the most dramatic form of change that an institution will ever experience.

The theme "from rags to riches" may well be applicable to the struggling college fortunate enough to attract and keep an outstanding leader as its president. A common, but perhaps less quoted observation is that of "from shirtsleeves to shirtsleeves in three generations." But either a business or an institution may fold or deteriorate under a single inept titular leader. These thoughts have some significance for institutions undergoing radical transitions, including that of presidential leadership, and will be discussed further. There are other, less dramatic and more subtle forms of transition which take place within an institution. It is appropriate that these be addressed as well.

METHODOLOGY OF TRANSITION

Everyone hopes for a smooth transition in the office of the president. The board hopes for this, the outgoing president hopes for it, and the internal constituencies hope for it. Although everyone hopes for this smooth transfer, few are able to say afterwards that it was satisfactory on all account books. This may not necessarily be traced to the procedures as planned, but to other psycho-social forces and influences. Nevertheless, it is appropriate to discuss proper transition procedures at this time.

It must be said at the outset that smoothness of transition depends upon a number of characteristics in the situation itself. If the outgoing president has been fired, or if he has departed early, there may be little opportunity for procedures to be arranged for an orderly transition. Of course, a few observers might suggest that this is the best of circumstances for the new president, but most consider an arranged form of change to be preferable. However, much depends upon the conditions under which the outgoing president is leaving as to how willing and helpful he may be to the incoming person.

New presidents should not be named too early. Most of the time, well organized and well intentioned boards and search committees may be concerned with setting a timetable which gives plenty of lead time for the new president to prepare to take office. While indeed this is helpful to that individual, and it is helpful to the institution which he leaves, it may divert the attention of those inside the institution from the business at hand, cause deferral of a number of matters until he comes on board, and make it more difficult for the outgoing president to continue his leadership role until the time set for change.

Generally speaking, selection procedures should be planned so that the new president is named approximately two months, no more than three months, prior to the time established for assuming official duties. This allows time for making personal adjustments and for orientation. The orientation period should not be considered as an overlapping of the two administrations. Only one person can be in charge. Although it may be helpful if the outgoing president continues to be available after his term expires, this tends to be more awkward for both parties. It is best for the orientation period to come before the new president takes office.

Immediately after the new president is named, he should begin receiving materials from the college. These should include current documents and material of future significance, as well as accumulated descriptive and planning documentation of the college. Examples might be the board's policies and procedures book, long range planning and facilities documents, audit reports, the most recent accreditation self studies and reports, budget and financial materials, and institutional research reports. The new president needs to do a lot of homework before he arrives for orientation; and every bit of information he receives should be taken seriously.

The suggested orientation period of one month need not be a full-time experience. In fact, two days a week is sufficient. This will allow the new president to wind down his present position while becoming acquainted with his new one. Concurrently, the outgoing president will have time to administer existing matters. During these days of orientation, the two presidents will need to spend many hours together. They need to explore every facet of operations jointly. If the circumstances of change are favorable, and if the two presidents establish a mutual rapport, this can become a very pleasant experience for both.

It is questionable how much conversation there should be about personnel between the outgoing and incoming administrations. There is something to be said for the new president forming his own judgments and opinions of personnel in order that the staff does not become the victim of a carryover form of negative bias. If such exchanges do occur, the outgoing president should confine his comments to statements strictly related to performance and refrain from personality descriptions. Also, it is well if the new president listens, but makes no firm judgments regarding the validity of these assessments until he has further confirmation.

Throughout the transition process, courtesy is the key. The outgoing president may introduce the new president to many different people, including presenting him formally to several assemblages. It is well if the former attempts to give these persons and groups a good impression of the new president in the manner he presents information about him. The outgoing president will also have many, many contexts in which he is asked about his successor. Professional courtesy dictates that his remarks be positive. A similar courtesy should be expected from the incoming president, who should always recognize the accomplishments of his predecessor.

The outgoing president should be sure that the new president meets the people he needs to know. These include influential persons in the community, local government personnel, some of his presidential colleagues, and the persons in state or other governmental and regulatory agencies with whom the college conducts business.

INSTITUTIONS IN TRANSITION

During periods when rapid change is occurring, whether it is a leadership transition or a short range and abrupt change, one tends to hear the expression, "This institution will never be the same again!" Usually this means that something good has been lost, or something disruptive has occurred. A college undergoing leadership changes will never be the same again, but this does not necessarily mean that things will be worse, nor does it mean that they will be better. It means that they will be different.

Subtle changes are always in process. The cast of characters in the drama changes as faculty come and go, board members come and go, and other posts change faces. The curriculum changes, teaching styles and technology change, and the student clientele is altered, but these are evolutionary changes. It is only when the major college positions, particularly those in academic leadership positions or the presidency, are undergoing a transition that change tends to become the central focus of attention.

Transitional states offer opportunities for progress. Unfortunately transitional states provide vulnerability to disaster as well. There is excitement associated with transitions, but there are also concomitant anxieties. What are some of these negative aspects of transitional change?

First, there is anxiety and uncertainty. Any disturbance of the equilibrium produces some tinge of anxiety, and larger disturbances tend to produce greater anxieties. Faculty and staff should indeed be concerned about local leadership changes, or other abrupt changes. However, they must guard against the tendency to become phobic, recognizing that what they are feeling is natural and, to some degree, realistic.

Second, transition can lead to tangential or erratic directional movement. Orderly movement through a transition demands that there be clear vision, a direction, and a course charted through the period and onward to the future. Those professional staff and others involved in guiding the change must recognize clearly where the college is headed or should be headed, and the goals toward which the whole movement is directed. Otherwise, there is drifting, or even worse, movement on a tangent away from true progress.

Third, transition exposes the institution to leadership error. Untried leadership is less predictable and more prone to error. Stable leadership tends to be conservative, while inexperienced leadership tends to be experimental. Leadership which is ill-fitted into the milieu can be disastrous.

Fourth, one of the three possible outcomes of transition is qualitative loss. There are bona fide hazards in change, and these should be recognized by all parties. Great caution must be exercised when tampering with success. Adjustments in one part of a system may produce stress in another. If the institution has inherent quality, the hazards of change are much greater.

Just as one outstanding leader may, over a period of time, transform an institution from an educational sow's ear into a silk purse, so may a poor leader allow, or even assist, a strong institution to drift or move erratically into deep trouble. The "rags to riches" theme has been acted out in higher education history, and so has the theme "from shirtsleeves to shirtsleeves in three generations," although in this case it may be only a single generation.

Fifth, there tends to be psycho-social disharmonies associated with transition. The stress associated with transitional change often disrupts staff relationships and may depress morale in general. Few changes are made without some opposition, and few changes are made without supporters. Extra care must be taken to avoid dissension during change.

However, transitional change is not without redeeming social and institutional values. It is well to recognize these also.

First, one of the three possible outcomes of transitional change is progress. Nothing remains static forever. Without progress there tends to be regression. Transitional change may be a part of institutional adaptation. Lessons learned from biological evolution have taught that the species which failed to adapt failed to survive. Colleges must adapt if they are to be survivors. Transitions offer opportunities to develop updated and improved versions of the former attributes.

Second, transitions may be revitalizing. Managed change can be stimulating with minimal anxiety. For many the status quo is either dull or unfulfilling of their potential. The excitement of transitional change can revitalize a complacent staff. Colleges tend to be plagued with some level of complacency, if not outright apathy, among staff. It is difficult to remain complacent during transitions, and it is foolish to be apathetic during such periods.

Third, transitions can be challenging. Transitions are demanding upon all those who are involved. Adaptation and adjustment requires extra effort. Meeting new demands requires greater effort. New leadership and new colleagues often require the re-establishment of one's past position of respect or recognition according to a somewhat different evaluative perspective. There is less security in resting upon one's laurels. Instead, one must earn new laurels in a changing environment.

Finally, transitions are necessary. Regardless of how individuals may feel about transition and change, and regardless of whether these are viewed to be progressive, they will nevertheless occur. These are the cycles of life in any social organization or institution. There will be a changing of the guard. There will also be a changing of the lieutenants, and even the captains of the guard. These things happen.

It has been said that the life cycle of an institution is one of birth, growth, maturity, and then either decline or renewal. Transition of leadership is irrelevant at the founding stage, but it can be highly critical during the growth and development stage. If the course of development has been properly charted, there must be continuity. Transition in leadership can be most traumatic in the mature institution, which has become somewhat stable and does not respond very well to the turbulence of change. In such instances, it is important to recognize that decline can be a result of stability if dynamics have slowed to a stage of near rigormortis. Transition in leadership offers an unusual opportunity for institutional renewal for the declining college.

Given all of the above, what should be the attitude of those inside constituencies of an institution in transition? What guidance may be offered regarding healthy responses to changing conditions?

First, remain positive. The secret weapon is one of attitude. If attitudes are positive, then perceptions will be open and most adaptive. If individuals close their perceptual fields toward the surrounding elements, then they will become the buffeted victims of change. It is important to remain optimistic.

Second, seize the opportunities available. Since transition brings change, it creates opportunities. Perceptions must remain open to these opportunities, and each individual must seize those which are within his reach and must join in a collective clutch of those that are within reach for the institution.

Third, become involved. Individual staff may influence the direction the transition takes and the general objectives toward which it is moving. Staff may be a part of the solutions rather than the problems of adjusting to changes within and without. Adaptation must become a group effort, not a task for a few.

Fourth, expect and even demand a managed form of transition. The staff has a right to expect that leadership changes will be handled properly and managed with the least disruption. Transition offers the opportunity to be better, but only if that opportunity is captured and skillfully executed will real progress occur.

Fifth, allow for an extension of pride. Individuals should not allow pride in the institution's past to restrict its opportunities, nor to overshadow its future. Once- glorious institutions have been known to stagnate in pride of the past. Although college constituencies may take legitimate pride in the accomplishments of the past and the current reputation which has been earned, this must not be blinding to opportunities nor stifling to progress. Pride must be found in today as well as yesterday. There must be pride in that which is yet to become.

THE INITIAL PERIOD

The first few months, or even year, of a new president's tenure have often been referred to as the "honeymoon" period. This is an apt description in many ways. It is a time when the president is just becoming acquainted. While there may be a number of persons who have adopted a "wait and see" attitude, he is likely to have no enemies and most will be anxious to make good impressions. No one really wants to be the first to try him by opposing his ideas, and any opposition is likely to be very diplomatic in character. There is a "feeling out" process on the part of the new president and of his internal constituent groups.

Some new presidents see the honeymoon period as a prime opportunity to make substantive changes, turning the institution's direction in a way which suits it, and to reshape and realign the internal organization. Actually there may be opportunities at this time for changes which will be more difficult to make in the future, but this approach may create additional disturbances which amplify the trauma of transition. Abrupt and substantive changes, while possibly attainable, may have lasting deleterious results, as well as tending to fragment or polarize the faculty and other internal groups.

In evaluating the wisdom of quick changes, much depends upon the condition of the college and its overall performance and quality level. If the institution enjoys the reputation of a quality academic institution which is reasonably well managed, then the new president is unwise to tamper too quickly with the systems in place. To do so not only invites resistance and criticism, but it exposes him immediately to evaluation of his professional judgments. If a change works out well, he may gain little. But if a change does not work out well, and the system in place was working satisfactorily, then not only is the credibility of his judgment dealt a blow, but also he may be seen as making change for the sake of change. Neither of these will aid in his future success.

Most new presidents would be well advised to take the system as it is, study it over a period of time to evaluate its functioning, and then decide what changes may be needed. This approach will allow the new president to avoid errors hurtful to him and to the college as well.

The new president should resist the temptation toward "flashy" changes. While these may be noticeable, they make little difference in the qualitative functioning of the institution. Often such changes are transparent to perceptive viewers, and suggest a certain shallowness in the new leader.

New presidents should be aware that there are always college staff members who have been chafing under perceived hardships for some time, and that there are those who have had ideas for different ways of functioning which have been rebuffed in the past. All of these pet ideas and all of these past frustrations, regardless of merit, tend to be loosed and paraded before the new president. Again, he will be wise to listen and evaluate these for a time before being overly influenced or committed to change.

New presidents tend to find themselves assailed from all sides by would-be advisors. The past president and members of the board have already loaded him with good advice. Then he arrives on the scene and his secretary, administrators, faculty, and even townspeople besiege him with more good advice. Some of this is indeed good advice, and some is not so good. The problem is one of differentiation. The new president should listen to all of it, and spend a lot of time in contemplation. He cannot afford to follow bad advice, since the responsibility for actions and decisions is his own.

Of course, one of the comments heard all too frequently, and perhaps to the point of irritation to the new president, is: "We have always done it this way." He should be patient and courteous in handling these situations. The new president will also be wise if he honors commitments made by the outgoing president. Some of these are institutional commitments and thus binding, but others may have been made to individuals. If these are official, it is necessary for them to be honored. To do otherwise invites *un*necessary criticism.

A word is in order about staffing close to the president. The likelihood is that he may inherit an efficient secretary. If so, this is indeed a blessing. A secretary familiar with people and the office traffic and routines can be invaluable to the new president. The new president should be cautious about making changes in those staff who serve him directly and those other administrators who are now a part of his team. These persons deserve the opportunity to work with him and to demonstrate that they can be an effective part of his organization. The possible reactions to sudden decisions concerning staff made by the new president will start his tenure on a sour note.

It may be noted that the repetitive theme in this advice for the new president is one of caution. The new president needs to go slowly. He needs to be careful and deliberate. However, he also needs to make those changes which in his judgment are critical to the well-being of the institution. In so doing, he may avoid fateful errors while providing some continuity and stability to an otherwise anxious social and psychological environment. Also, he begins with a desirable reputation as being a president who is not impetuous, but rather studied and considerate in actions which affect others. If he has a developing agenda for the institution, it will not be lost through this approach, and success in reaching goals is likely to be augmented by patience.

Topics for Discussion or Further Study

1. Develop a rationale supporting the author's suggested period of orientation with the outgoing and incoming presidents; or, suggest a different period and timing and provide a rationale for your suggestion.

2. Why is a transition laden with both opportunities and dangers for an institution?

3. What is your best advice to an incoming president in an institution with which you are familiar?

4. Has the author been excessive in urging caution about abrupt changes during the "honeymoon" period? Give an example of a situation in which this may be good advice, and give an example of a situation in which less caution would be appropriate.

5. The author cautions against "flashy" changes, or what might be termed "making a splash." Give examples of the highly visible changes to which he may be referring.

PART TWO

Effective Presidential Leadership

CONSTITUENCIES

5

The president must work with a number of different constituency groups. Depending upon the detail of classification, these may range from four to over a hundred or more. For purposes of simplification, only four basic constituencies will be discussed in any detail. These are faculty, students, regents, and the general public.

FACULTY

It is difficult to rank these constituencies in order of significance. It would be correct to say that the president must first solidify himself internally, and remain solid internally, to have the necessary support base to meet the challenges he must face externally. Speaking strictly in terms of the significance of the relationship, priority must be given to the faculty constituency.

Most presidents have their origins as faculty members. It is well that this never be forgotten by the president or faculty. When identifying himself publicly by means of a reference group, the president should stress his role as faculty leader. He must convey to the faculty that he perceives his professional identity as being one of them who happens to have a broader assignment. Regents, students, and the public should be led to see the president as an academician, a scholar, and professorial in character and traits. This is a highly respectable, professional identity, and one which fits well into the presidential image.

Having once identified himself as mutant faculty person, the president must frequently demonstrate, as well as articulate, this identity. Since the purpose of his institution is teaching and learning, he should not find it difficult to focus upon interests in common with the faculty. Among other considerations, this means that the president must continue his interest in curricular and instructional matters. He must continue to be interested in academic standards, and in the conditions under which teaching and learning occur.

Professional courtesy is extremely important. By the manner in which the president deals with faculty, others are led to attribute the proper respect which is due these academicians. Faculty should receive respect when dealing with all campus offices. Support staff must be led to see their role as one of carrying on all of the necessary adjunct tasks so that faculty may concentrate on teaching. Throughout the institution there must be an understanding that the central processes are those of teaching and learning.

It has been observed that faculty activism is almost a predictable phenomenon. Since most faculty hold advanced degrees, it goes without statement that this group is constituted by extremely intelligent people whose abilities for the most part are under-utilized. After spending month after month and year after year teaching the same lower division undergraduate courses, it is to be expected that faculty will search for other means of self-fulfillment and actualization of talents. Under what other conditions and in what other professions can there be found a group of such able people with so little control of their own destiny?

For psychological reasons, if for no other, faculty must be given a meaningful role in internal institutional governance. They must see themselves as professionals, and they cannot have such a perception if they encounter difficulties in their necessary relationships with administrative offices. This is not to say that faculty should be regarded as a group of "prima donnas" whose whims should have catering, nor should any such behaviors be tolerated. It simply means that professional respect should be extended, and professional respect expected in return.

Perhaps a word is in order regarding communications. Having visited many campuses as an accrediting evaluator, this writer has found relatively few on which communications between administration and faculty were considered good. There were, however, a number on which communications were considered by faculty to be poor. This may reflect the psychology suggested above. In truth, it may be stated that faculty are rarely pleased with communications, sometimes for good cause and sometimes not.

It is well that the president make a vow never to allow the faculty to read important news in the media, campus or other, as an initial way of being informed. An internal memorandum, newsletter, or specially called meeting are effective means to give such information directly. A personal presentation in a meeting, however hastily called, is preferable for delicate or highly significant institutional developments.

Regular forms of communication, such as monthly meetings and intervening news memos are very important. Faculty need to know the significant happenings which may impact in some way upon them. In times of particular anxiety, the president may schedule several hours of small group "communication sessions" for interaction with faculty.

The president's door should always be open to any faculty member. This is not to say that the faculty member may not later be referred to the proper dean or division chair to pursue the matter further, but the president must be willing to listen and make the referral. He must be willing to listen to faculty as they tell him of their important achievements, or state their problems and concerns. If an injustice can be righted informally and a grievance avoided, that informal process can be started.

The president should accept and enjoy the role of counselor when members of his faculty bring him their professional problems and career aspirations. Counseling, advising, and mentoring relationships are indicators of positive personal and professional relationships, and should be so viewed.

Administrators are often viewed by faculty as being more concerned with buildings, budgets, and public relations than they are with people. They are sometimes considered as the enemies of academic standards, since they may on occasion find it necessary to deal with a faculty member who is overly stringent in grading or unrealistic in the amount of work required of students. Within the philosophical context of the community college, the president must lead his administrative team to retain their concerns with student academic performance and with the demonstration of suitable collegiate evaluation and grading systems.

Faculty have a legitimate interest in the maintenance of an academically well-qualified peer group, and the assignment of courses to instructors who are properly credentialed. The president must see that academic traditions and standards are protected throughout the institution. Assignments of courses must not capriciously ignore faculty favorites. Even though this task may be delegated to the academic administrator, the president must set the tone.

The president may find it easier to relate to faculty if he continues scholarly interests and pursuits. Although it is difficult to find time to teach a course, he may do so on occasion. He should have some identity in his academic field, perhaps attending a meeting or conference in that area from time to time with faculty members.

It may seem a small matter, but it is highly important that the president defer at times to the expertise of faculty in their own area of study. The president must be cautious of preempting faculty judgments in their own curricular field. The president, in pursuing matters of purely academic curiosity or of professional concern, should ask the opinions of faculty or request technical information and advice from faculty on these matters of intellectual interest in their respective fields of expertise.

It is unfortunate that in many institutions the most natural relationships between the president and the faculty have become limited and restrained by rigidities associated with collective bargaining, negotiations, and contracts. Sometimes these create bottlenecks in communication, problem resolution, and professional interaction. While in some sectors these must be accepted as a part of the social and professional environment of the institution, it is desirable that professionalism be allowed to transcend such arrangements where feasible.

STUDENTS

While direct interactions with students are limited, and it is wise that these be limited, the president must be visible on campus. Students must see that he is a reality, not a mythical figure in a back office planning new buildings and juggling finances. The president should attend activities, greet students on campus, meet with smaller groups, and be accessible to students with problems.

It is not suggested that the president put on casual clothes and sit informally with students in mixers or the student union coffee shop. The relationship is essentially that of faculty leader to student, and it is a professional one in character. Too much familiarity is inappropriate.

Students must see the president as a real person who has their interest and welfare at heart. Campus media can be utilized in building this image. However, it is surprising how much students notice, and how the campus grapevine works with either good or bad messages. This writer once danced with a handicapped girl, who had been less than popular as a partner, at a campus function. It seemed the right thing to do. The message made the campus rounds with a positive effect completely unanticipated. While most such acts attract little known attention, the president must realize that students are observing and making judgments.

The president must take the position that any rule or policy can be explained and justified to students who are open-minded and willing to understand. He must also take the position that any campus rule which cannot be justified should be changed. This attitude needs to extend to others, particularly to student personnel administrators and other campus offices dealing directly with students. Further, the president must assist in developing sensitivity among those who communicate with students. Communications (and rules) are often tersely stated so as to be offensive.

Sometimes a rule or procedure, arranged for the convenience of staff or office routine, creates problems for students. When such instances come to the attention of the president, most often via student complaints, the president must initiate adjustments. Students must perceive the president as being willing to consider such matters, and they must know that his office is open to them when satisfaction has not been obtained at the lower echelons.

When an appeal is made to the president regarding a decision of a personnel dean, the student must expect that the appeal will receive its deserved attention from that office. Students must not have the attitude and belief that an appeal is an exercise in futility since the president always backs subordinates. While indeed that may tend to be the result, the president must listen to the student, examine the circumstances, and make his own judgment.

For a reversal of a subordinate's ruling, or a hearing committee's judgment, there must be good and sufficient reason. These persons have considered the case in more detail than the president is likely to have time to devote. Nevertheless, many such appeals are extremely important to students and must be taken seriously. When it appears that the student has been treated unfairly, a reversal is in order. More frequently the student may have been treated summarily or arbitrarily and remanding the case for reconsideration may be the appropriate action.

Some attention should be given to proper appeals of academic grievances, such as grading. This is usually handled by the academic administrator, and perhaps a faculty or faculty-student committee. In appeals coming from such a body, the president must protect academic standards and the right of faculty to evaluate, but at the same time he must not side with whimsical or capricious treatment of students or with bias in a hearing body controlled by other faculty.

The president must monitor the athletic program of the college, keeping it within prescribed guidelines of the institution and the athletic associations with which the college is affiliated. While there are many zones of quicksand around and within which the president must maneuver, this is one of the more hazardous ones. It goes without saying that athletics must be kept under institutional control, and under the supervision and direction of the college administration. Booster groups and others must not be allowed to operate unfettered, and coaches and other personnel must be accountable internally rather than externally. Athletics must be kept in a proper perspective within the institution.

Perhaps a discussion of the administrative problems of athletics is not totally germane to the topic of relationships with students, but it is an area where the interests of the president and a large segment of the student body meet. The president should be the number one fan of the college's teams, and should be seen as such by the athletes and student fans. These activities, as well as others which are less public, are excellent opportunities for the president and his family to be visible and seen as sharing some common interests with students.

Other groups with which the president should take an especially active role are the honors organizations. The president should be a frequent guest at Phi Theta Kappa functions. He should be a listed cosponsor of the scholars club made up of those students who earn the grade point to qualify for his honor roll. If the college has an academic quiz-bowl team, or if it sponsors events of that nature, the president should take an active interest.

The president's relationships with student government should be once removed. That is, this function falls within the province of the student personnel staff and a sponsor from that division. However, it is well that the president attend student government meetings at the beginning of each new year, giving both an orientation and encouragement to their work. An occasional brief appearance to discuss a matter of common interest is always fruitful. He should also be available to student leaders who wish to discuss problems or special activities with him. It is well on such occasions that the president receive prior briefing from the student personnel staff, or he may sometimes defer decision or action on a matter until he receives input from that sector.

GOVERNING BOARD

The governing board may be considered either an internal or an external constituency. Since they represent public involvement, accountability, and control, they may at times appear to be an external constituency. This image is fostered by their lack of a regular presence on campus. However, the successful president must lead his regents (trustees) to see themselves as an internal constituency. Regardless of their method of arrival in office, through appointment or election, regents should recognize themselves as an integral part of the institution. Their role is different. It is one of oversight and policy making. But this role is vital to the internal workings of the college.

Along this same line, governing board members must be led to view their loyalty obligations as being to the welfare of the college.

Some board members may have been elected with the aid and assistance of some particular group or external constituency, and it may be difficult for them to set this identity aside. Board members may have been appointed by the governor of the state, perhaps as a result of political affiliation and campaign activity, and these associations may be difficult to ignore. However, once the board member takes the oath of office, his legal and ethical obligations are clearly to public service as a general overseer of the affairs of the institution.

Essentially, the board has two functions. One is to see that policies which assure that the institution fulfills its proper role in service to the public are enacted and followed. The other is to exercise general oversight of the public's interests and property in terms of accountability and fiduciary control of funds and property. While certainly more extensive listings are appropriately made, and often enacted into law, it is very important that the board members understand these two generic functions to be basic and essential to their role.

It is easy for those in academia to see themselves as a part of a somewhat independent, self-directing, perpetuated entity which is publicly sustained because of its obvious value and beauty. The president must counteract such tendencies, fostering instead a view of the college as a service organization dedicated to the public welfare and accountable to the public.

Some regents are easier to work with than others, and occasionally it is necessary to have a private conference with a board member to correct some misconception of role or a behavior which was disturbing to the equilibrium of the institution and to working relationships. Providing board members come to their duties with a reasonably open mind and with honorable intentions, schisms and conflicts of a severe nature are seldom necessary.

It is the obligation of the president to give the board a proper orientation to their role and to educate them about institutional affairs. It is best that the orientation be given personally, but parts may be through vicarious means including conference meetings, shared orientation with other boards in the region, readings, and video materials. The board's own operational manual should spell out in some detail the duties of the board and the relationships of the board with administrative and other personnel.

The principles of proper board functioning have been the subject of several books and numerous articles. The discussion here is not intended to be exhaustive, but rather to hit the high spots of coverage in significant areas.

Normally, the statutes or other legal framework charges the board with extensive responsibilities for the institution. It should be realized, and statutes themselves often recognize the fact, that the board cannot possibly perform all the duties and responsibilities it is assigned. Frequently, these are delegated to the college administration, headed by the president. It has been said that the most important act of the board is the employment of a president, and then it must back off and let the president run the institution. That is an oversimplification, of course, but delegation of duties and authority is necessary to the proper functioning of the enterprise.

It has also been said that the board's function is policy making and the president's function is policy administration, and that each should stay strictly within the designated province. This, too, is overly simplified. In truth, the president sometimes makes internal policies, and often he prepares policy, or endorses and brings policy recommended by others to the board for adoption.

Certainly, the board should not be left to write its own policies nor should members be expected to have knowledge of all the areas in which policy is needed. It is the role of the president to advise and recommend policy to the board. If the board sees the need for policy in a given area, it directs the president to prepare and bring policy recommendations to it. As mentioned earlier, the board also has a fiduciary function to the public for both the operation and the fiscal functioning of the college, and these are oversight rather than policy making activities.

The board employs personnel only upon the recommendation of the president. The only exceptions to this rule should be the legal advisor, architects, and auditors. Even in these areas the president should have opportunity for input. If legal restrictions allow, the board should delegate to the president the employment of adjunct, temporary, and part-time personnel such as student workers, without board sanction. The employment of other full-time personnel should be official only after board approval, but these actions should be perfunctory unless there is some unusual circumstance or problem.

The board should deal with personnel through the president. If there are problems, these should be brought to the president's attention for handling. Any other institutional personnel presenting information or reporting to the board should be at the president's invitation. Of course, it is wise for the president to allow the business officer to present reports, as well as the academic officer and others as needs arise. It is well also for the board to visit various offices and departments on occasion. Such visits should be arranged by the president so that the board can see and hear directly from staff what is transpiring in each department and what some of the needs of that area are. Routine, periodic reporting may be scheduled for numerous campus leaders and groups, including student government, faculty elected leaders, and division heads.

Within any legal guidelines and board policies which may have been adopted, the president and his staff should be authorized to do purchasing and conduct other business affairs of the college. Board or legal guidelines should establish procedures and set limits for this authority, and a periodic reporting system should be required. This reporting system should constantly assure the board that expenditures are within the parameters of budgeting, and audits should verify financial statements and accounts as well as assure the board that guidelines and good business practices are being followed. Of course, only the board purchases or disposes of real estate, but only on the recommendation of the president.

The president is the advisor and the executive officer of the board. He serves as the public spokesperson for the board, except on certain occasions when the chairperson also assumes such a role. Each board member cannot and should not attempt to speak for the board. The board acts only as a group and only in official meeting. Members must refrain from involving themselves individually in the affairs of the college or in matters dealing with individual college personnel. If a board member comes on campus to obtain information or make observations, that member should check in with the president who will make arrangements and assist the member in gaining the understanding sought. Staff must be accountable to the administration and the president, and they must not become confused as to whom they should report.

Except when matters pertaining to his own performance and employment are being considered, the president should always be present at board meetings.

When ignorance or ill will threatens the institution or any element of it, the governing board should be available for support. In grave crises, the governing board will be expected to serve in the role of champion for the president and the college. The board should understand that the protection it offers is a fundamental defense of the vested interest of society in its educational institutions.

Since community and junior college boards are often from the community or the vicinity, members will have more knowledge about the institution than other collegiate boards. They will have more exposure to community comment, complaints from faculty, and complaints from students. They will also hear of successes, which may or may not be the most significant ones on campus. Board members should act as a buffer for insignificant and petty complaints and gossip. If a member evaluates a person's complaint to be of some significance, he should refer that person to the president for investigation of the complaint and subsequent action.

The board should function as a committee of the whole. This is to say, the board should resist the temptation to form committees within its membership. Committees tend to assume the authority of the entire board. The board itself tends not to offend committees by rejecting or altering their recommendations, thus allowing the committee to act in its behalf by default. Oftentimes the board may be hearing a recommendation for action from one of its committee chairs when it should expect such recommendations to come from its president.

The board should discipline its own members and not leave this to the president. If a member is out of line, or crosses the bounds of courtesy, ethics, or the guidelines set by the board for the conduct of its affairs, then the other members should bring direct pressures to bear on that member. Members must not refrain in courtesy to another member while the president or any other employee is bullied or subjected to unfair treatment.

Occasionally, the board will encounter a member who fancies himself as an expert on collegiate education because he holds a degree or two. Once in a while, a board member becomes an expert on business management and budgeting as a result of operating a private business. A publisher tends to be an expert on the education of journalists and graphic arts specialists. It is true that members have special expertise and may at times be asked to contribute from that knowledge. However, caution must be taken lest these members make both administrative and teaching staff uncomfortable in their work.

It is important that the board have a properly detailed policy statement on the conduct of its meetings. There should be no confusion as to how an item gets on the agenda, who is allowed to address the board during meetings, or on any other matter of the same nature. Deviations should be few, under very unusual circumstances, and should require unanimous consent, including that of the president.

In spite of all of these pitfalls, most boards function surprisingly smoothly. Many members sense these areas of concern, or quickly become educated on them and adapted to them. It is helpful if the board is on record with policy statements governing their own ethical conduct. This makes it easier for another member, or even the president, to point toward contemplated or present actions which may not be in conformity.

It is difficult to set a value on the services rendered by public spirited citizens who serve on governing boards. Good board members are worth their weight in gold, if not in some more precious substance. These people give of their time and energies, and often expose themselves to criticisms, verbal attacks, and bad publicity, as well as legal liability, in order to perform a public service. Presidents and others within the institution should keep this in mind, and should extend recognition, courtesies, and credit to board members in every reasonable fashion.

THE PUBLIC

While the public may at times be a single individual, most often the public consists of organized groups. These may be official in nature such as local or state government entities or elected officials with responsibilities which relate to the conduct of educational activities directly or indirectly. Sometimes the public organizes itself into support groups beneficial to the college. Occasionally, special interest groups are organized for the purpose of change, curtailment, resistance, or control. The president must deal effectively with such groups. He must do so under the assumption that all groups have positive intentions, even though some may be misguided as to how to accomplish their mission.

The best preparation for dealing with pressure groups with special interests is to have procedures in place for their input into the system. It is also useful to have in mind, and in writing, the institution's position on any anticipated issues. Policies are best adopted prior to a crisis, since few good policies are made during turmoil.

As an example, every college should have a policy governing library acquisitions and the display of the collection. This may seem unimportant until a local "book burner" group becomes active and begins to make demands for the removal of certain publications from the collection. However, the existence of a board approved policy covering this issue protects and relieves the president and his staff as they move to meet such a controversy.

A pressure group cannot be allowed to badger the institution into taking a stance opposing its mission, creating hardship for others, changing a tenet of its philosophy, or departing from its philosophy in its practice. It is the president's (and the board's) duty to convey these basics as discussions are held. While diplomacy is important, candor (even stubbornness) is acceptable in such circumstances. Institutional personnel and board members must be prepared to enunciate patiently over and over again the institution's basic philosophical orientation and its broad general purposes.

Some institutions find a proportionally large minority within their service area and, accordingly, they attempt to offer educational programs to meet the needs of that clientele. While it is entirely appropriate to do this, it may not be that simple.

These needs seen as evident by members of the predominant ethnic group making up the institution's staff may not be the same as the needs as seen by members of the minority. Although certain moves and adaptations on the part of the college may be appropriate in any such circumstance, it is well to establish communications and dialogue with ethnic group leadership prior to embarking on broad program initiatives.

Also, it must be realized that within minority constituencies there are factions. Whenever the opportunity exists for establishing official communications, it is best if these are established with the titular leadership within the minority, if such exists, rather than with a faction selected by or making itself known to college authorities.

The writer's college served a geographic region in which there were six Native American tribes. From hard experience, it was learned that contacts should be made with each current tribal chairman, allowing them to designate liaison council members to work with the college. It was learned also that it was best to establish relationships and to perform services which were testaments to the sincerity of the college's interest, and then allow these groups to bring their needs to the institution rather than postulating them unilaterally. Minorities tend to be unimpressed by words of non-minority leaders which are unsupported by past actions.

A further word of caution is in order. This regards the purposes of the institution as related to the demands made upon it from various constituencies of the public. The functions of community and junior colleges have been set forth clearly in numerous sources, from law itself to college catalogs and the professional literature. The college is an educational institution and not a social welfare agency. It is not responsible for the failures of society at large, nor is its function to serve youth below a prescribed age. The resources of the college must be committed to educational programs for its own clientele and to fulfill its defined mission and purposes. Its energies and its resources must not be dissipated in other social causes however worthy these may be.

MANAGING CONFLICT

It is important to note that while the president must recognize and develop skills in dealing with various constituencies, all involving some complications, the real problems come when there is a conflict between and among these constituency groups. Some student proposals are opposed by faculty or would arouse general opposition if adopted. Some proposals of faculty may be unacceptable to regents, or are likely to provoke public response and perhaps hostility among students. Some demands of public bodies may be foreign to the value systems of faculty, and some are sure to arouse the ire of students.

The president must rarely espouse a special cause of any one of his basic constituent groups which will alienate him from another. Instead, the president must balance the concerns of each, frequently reminding one group of another's position. At times he must be persuasive in explaining why a given proposal will not be acceptable, and why it must be modified or abandoned. He must explain what changes must be made in the proposal in order for it to receive his endorsement and recommendation. Above all, he must avoid duplicity. He cannot talk from different sides with each group separately.

If the president has a position of his own which he firmly believes to be correct, and if the issue is a significant one, then he should so state and stay with this position in all discussions. In this case, he may find himself allied with one constituency against another, but only as a result of a common perception on an issue important to the institution.

The president may allow a group to advocate its own proposals through the appropriate channels without endorsement. Or, at times the president may "coach" one constituency group on how to modify its proposals in order to win his approval or the support and endorsement of others. Working between and among these constituency groups, keeping each with some modicum of satisfaction, and alienating none, constitutes one of the principal challenges to presidential skills. How well he handles this challenge is a standard measure of his success.

Topics for Discussion or Further Study

1. The author characterizes faculty as a group whose intellectual abilities are under-utilized, and explains tendencies toward activism with this as one explanation. Do you agree? Take a position and defend it.

2. What methods or procedures may be utilized to enhance two-way communications between administration and faculty.

3. What methods or procedures may be utilized effectively for communications between administration and students? What hazards are involved and what cautions are appropriate?

4. What should the president's role be in the appeals process for student grievances?

5. In a case situation where the board has undertaken to enact a policy regulating faculty in a way with which the president disagrees but must enforce, what should be the president's course of action and response.

6. How does the board serve as a political buffer for the college?

7. Does the president have a role in correcting a board member's conduct when it is viewed as disruptive to the proper functioning of the college?

8. Who has the responsibility for orientation and education of new board members? What are some of the procedures?

9. From experience or from the literature, prepare a brief case summary of a situation where an off-center special interest group has challenged policies or practices of an institution in an inappropriate fashion, and provide an analysis and critique of the manner in which the situation was handled.

10. Give an example of a circumstance when the positions of faculty, students, and parents (public) may challenge the management skills of the administration.

GOVERNANCE

6

INTERNAL GOVERNANCE

In today's academic climate, any presidential candidate who disavows a belief in the principle of shared governance is unlikely to be elected to that post. Any current president who disclaims a commitment to the principle is likely to be branded as an authoritarian, a despot, or worse. Further, any president who does not recognize the values inherent in the utilization of the pool of human resources within the institution in shaping and developing its future is guilty of foolishness or stupidity, or both. Therefore, any questions as to the wisdom and the appropriateness of extending to the professional staff a voice and a share in institutional self-determination may be dispensed and the discussion turned to systems and degrees of participation in internal governance.

Official Institutional Structure

The reference here to official institutional structure is synonymous with the meaning normally attributed to "the chain of command." In the downward direction in the academic sector, this is the one which begins with the president, proceeds through the chief academic officer to the division or department heads, and on to the faculty. Other professionals and support staff presumably have a similar pathway.

Oftentimes, the official institutional structure is either ignored or dismissed as a form of shared governance. Usually it is viewed, especially by faculty, as a means of supervision and control. And indeed it has this purpose. However, those who fail to recognize this structure as a part of the shared governance system are looking at the system strictly in the top to bottom sequence, and overlooking the fact that it can function from bottom to top.

The structure provides a communications system which works both ways. Institutional leadership may use the structure to exert leadership force and direction within the institution, and faculty may use the system to communicate their ideas and their concerns upward.

In theory, an institution with a perfectly working structure might never need other forms of governance. But, alas, such is not the case. While the structure works reasonably well for certain purposes, it works less well for others. It cannot escape the stigma of "the chain of command" among faculty members who will continue to see it as the span of control rather than the funnel for input.

There is also validity to the criticism that the official structure is a pyramid which reaches downward in a linear fashion but does not provide for lateral communications and interaction. This is to say that while members of a given department or division may make their collective thinking known upward through the chair, it does not provide for members of various divisions to format their collective thinking and make it known to the upper echelons.

For these and similar reasons, no institution should expect to rely on its formal and official organizational structure to function properly as the only means of shared participation in governance. However, the potential which lies within the structure should not be ignored, and the system should be made to function as a two-way communications linkage.

Participative Governance Systems

Surely the earliest of this century's participative systems in colleges and universities must be the faculty committee system. It has a checkered history of effectiveness and ineffectiveness both in terms of output and participation. Nevertheless, the faculty committee system may have the greatest potential of all for meaningful involvement of professional staff in the affairs of the college.

There are certain requirements for a committee system to work effectively. First, committees must have a definite function or charge. They must know what they are to be about in the way of business, and they must know to whom they report in order for action to be taken or changes wrought. Secondly, there must be active participation by the members. Committee members must be motivated by the belief that their function is a significant one, and that their recommendations will be heard and have some potential of progressing into changes.

Faculty committees may have official status within the institution or they may not. Perhaps at this point some digression is appropriate, with a return to discussion of committees later.

For years, the popular form of faculty participation has tended to bear the designation of "faculty association." Usually the faculty association has been an organization of the full-time instructional staff members, with a constitution spelling out structure and purposes which was submitted through the administration to the board for review and approval.

These organizations have appeared at times to be primarily focused on issues of faculty welfare. When they are more broadly spread in their scope of interests, they have tended to initiate committees and to perform functions similar to those of institutional committees. Sometimes duplicate committees are found with one set reporting to the association and the other to the college administration.

While almost any institutional governance system which offers meaningful participation for professional staff will work in an atmosphere of professionalism and good will, some styles are better than others. The separate and independent faculty association system has merits, not the least of which is that it offers a forum for discussion, debate, and recommendations independent of administrative intimidation or threat. This same characteristic may make it less effective as a change agent within the institution. Nevertheless, it may be made to work well by determined leadership within the faculty and the administration.

It is suggested that study and consideration be given to the logic that the best shared governance system is one which provides for: (1) a single set of committees which serve both the needs of professional staff and the institution; (2) opportunity for percolation, or more direct upstreaming, of ideas from the professional staff to those who must approve and implement them; (3) a forum in which both ideas and concerns may be discussed independent of administration; (4) membership from all the professional staff on campus, including counselors, librarians, student affairs staff, and even other administrators; and (5) professional staff representation on the body which acts in a basic advisory role to the president. If this logic is accepted, and if one can escape the term and definition of "faculty association," then there is hope of forming a participative system within the institution which does all of the above.

This new creature may be called any suitable title, even the generic one of "institutional professional participative system" will work. It may have its own constitution and by-laws, and its committees are those of the institution itself. This latter point is of considerable significance in certain areas where committees act on behalf of the college. In almost every college there are committees which administer certain college events and functions and which act as official hearing groups in matters of student discipline, academic probation and suspension, traffic appeals, grievances, and the like. It is questionable whether any groups other than official college committees can be authorized to perform these functions and make these judgments and decisions on behalf of the institution.

Following this logic the organization's constitution should provide for the titular leadership of the institution and of its academic sector to occupy central ex-officio positions. However, it must also provide for a role with rank for an elected professional staff member, and it must provide for the election of those representatives who will occupy slots on the president's advisory council along with certain principal administrators. Committee assignments should reflect individual choice, recommendation of the elected faculty leader, and sanction by the chief academic officer and the president. If committees are to act on behalf of the college, these must be constituted by official appointment.

An important feature to any such institutional professional participative system is that of a representative caucus group which meets independent of the administration, discusses innovations and concerns, and communicates those about which there is consensus to the appropriate administrative office or the committee with an assigned function in the topical area. This caucus group should be formed by: the elected leader and the elected representatives to the president's advisory council; elected representatives from the committees dealing with faculty welfare, academic standards, and student affairs; and one elected representative of the division chairs and an elected representative of administrators at the level of assistant dean, director, or coordinator. In order to preserve anonymity and confidentiality, this group should keep no minutes, only a record of agreed upon outcomes or recommendations.

This discussion of an institutional professional participative system has been in considerable conceptual detail. It is essential that colleges not abandon the search for a structure which will embody the essential features of the faculty association mode while still retaining the values of the structural design of the official system within the institution. Although systems based upon the concept as outlined above are known to work effectively, any system's effectiveness depends on the people involved. The faculty and the administration must understand the system, and it requires a constant educational and motivational effort in order to function properly. But, then, so does any other such system.

Perspective

The gradual erosion of the authority of titular leadership in many higher education institutions has left them without an effective balancing system. There is little assurance of stable and orderly change, and there is little assurance of equity or justice under known and recognized collegiate values and principles. More frequent than the near-anarchy so often cited in the popular and professional literature, there is a fragmentation of the effective forces in the institution into factions. The social techniques of this polarized educational society have become confrontation and negotiation. The power tactics traditional in the world diplomacy of the past are brought into play.

There are many versions of how this state of educational and societal affairs has been reached. Some have pointed out that democracy has built into it the means of its own destruction, and that there is a fuse burning. On a more optimistic note, it should be said that democracy also embodies the means of its own salvation and renewal.

There is little doubt that the day of benevolent despotism has passed. Few mourn its demise. Paternalism has become out of place and obsolescent, although some seek to hold on to a few of its values, including familial identity, responsibility to others, human compassion, and mutual support. Some miss the quality of authoritarian finality that once characterized the presidential office as they are buffeted by the uncertainties that characterize the environment in a number of institutions.

It seems unlikely that in the immediate future the chief administrator will avoid accepting responsibility for the effective operation of the institution's many, and often unrelated, programs and enterprises, regardless of to whom they have been assigned or the relative absence of his active personal involvement in them. Delegation of duties is much more simple than delegation of responsibility.

Nevertheless, there must be a delegation of decision-making authority, and there must be a dispersion of innovative initiative. Any higher education institution would soon become the victim of its own life processes if it failed to provide for these. The survival failure of certain of earth's creatures with inadequate neural systems stresses the necessity of proper internal communications. The failure of still others with exoskeleton support sounds a warning against the rigid encrustation of administrative processes and procedures, and suggests the value of a strong, but resilient and growing, internal support structure.

In the search for a new, but meaningful and effective, role for administration, the key may be found in the areas of philosophy, principles, values, and the situation ethics of the college environment. There is still a place for charisma, although few possess the qualities to lead merely by force of personality. Too frequently fertile ideas are awash in the competitive intellectual sea characteristic of college environments.

There must be a singular guiding force within any viable institution if it is to avoid the pits into which so many appear to have fallen. While the values of participation of faculty, other staff, students, and even the public, in institutional processes go unquestioned, there must be a welding process which unifies all these elements. The techniques of administration may of necessity change, but these must enable it to fulfill this role to be effective in preserving the goals inherent in moving the institution in a unified direction.

In the search for the techniques attendant to this new role, many administrators will experience problems of adaptation. Staff will experience similar problems. Unless a clear understanding and an acceptance of the obligations of professionalism emerges, systems will flounder in confusion. Strong leadership, whether authoritative or participative in nature, will continue to be a necessary ingredient in the orderliness and stability of colleges and universities, as well as in their progress.

EXTERNAL GOVERNANCE

Governance Systems

Public community colleges across the land function under various systems of external governance, normally dependent upon the legal milieu prescribed under applicable state enactments. In most states there is an *institutional governing board*, which is responsible for one college or sometimes several. A second tier of governance is often found in a *state coordinating board*, which normally has certain specific coordinative powers over all institutions within the state. However, in some states there is an intermediary body which functions as a *state community college board*, having defined authority over all two-year colleges, which may or may not be subservient in various ways to another state board with broader responsibilities.

For example, the state of Oklahoma has a mixture of boards. Some governing boards are responsible for a single institution, while other governing boards have not only multiple institutions within their purview of authority but also institutions of different types, such as a comprehensive university, four-year baccalaureate universities, and two-year colleges. In Oklahoma there is a state coordinating board with broad powers over such areas as fund division, degrees and credentials, and admission standards.

The state of Minnesota has one state governing board with broad powers over all of its two-year colleges. The chancellor of this system and his staff wield a pervasive influence on the operations of the entire system. Local colleges have only advisory citizen boards which have very limited powers of a recommending nature, and sometimes little actual influence.

In Illinois there are locally elected governing boards for community colleges and a relatively strong state junior college board. There is a coordinating board with very limited powers. Colorado has local advisory boards with a state junior college board having developing strength. The legislature there exercises rather strong controls over institutions with a budget bill, appropriately called "the long bill" since it may be approximately a foot thick. In Kansas locally elected boards are coordinated by the State Board of Education which also governs both the public schools and the vocational school system.

These examples, somewhat oversimplified, are given as illustrations of the variety of external governance situations under which two-year colleges must function in fulfilling their respective missions. Perhaps there is not one "best" governance system, but certainly some provide a better environment for local institutions to function at an optimum level than others. It is surprising that quality institutions are able to perform effectively under various governance system handicaps. Also, it may be noted that there are institutions functioning poorly under what might be considered by some as ideal governance systems.

As these affect institutional operations, governance systems may be evaluated according to certain functional criteria. These may include: the provision of opportunity for the institution to be responsive to local needs and conditions, allowance of sufficient autonomy for local leadership to function creatively, insulation of the college from political interference, and the provision of policies and conditions of service for all professional staff to perform educational functions effectively.

Other criteria might be used in evaluating the effectiveness of a higher level of state governance. These might, at least in part, address the system's ability to: resist political intervention; protect the public from inferior or sham collegiate operations; practice advocacy and lobbying effectiveness in obtaining resources, assessing institutional needs, and dividing funds according to acceptable measures of work load and performance; assure free movement of students within the system of institutions and tier levels; clarify role definitions among governing boards; and assure the public of accountability and stewardship of resources and human potential.

If the writer were to attempt a recitation of current problems in governance systems, these would most certainly include: the tendency to magnify the regulatory function while minimizing the advocacy function; a movement toward increasing state regulation at the expense of institutional autonomy; and a tendency toward concentration of power at the state level at the expense of institutional governance.

Governance and Coordination

Governance is principally the responsibility of the institutional governing board. In the opinion of the writer, this can best be accomplished at the local level by a single board for the institution. Absentee governing boards know too little about the actual functioning of the college, and must depend upon the information provided by the president or upon informal (and often critical) communications from activist members of various campus constituencies. Formal liaisons of the absentee board with campus advisory committees of faculty and student constituencies are laden with peril, and tend to undermine presidential authority. Public advisory committees are often an exercise in futility since they have little power and no legally assigned duties, and tend to constitute challenges for the president to manage in any positive way.

Since many community colleges depend upon local property tax levies for a portion of their funding, and some even have legal authority to set required millage within limits, it seems appropriate that board members be elected by the voting public in such situations. While elected boards are a prime example of democracy in action when they function properly, these often present problems when certain influences become paramount in elections and in deliberations. The writer has observed boards which functioned primarily as tax-payer protective committees, and owed allegiance to such activists through election support. Further, the writer has observed elected boards dominated by teacher union representatives from the public school sector, members of the same union which represents the faculty in collective bargaining. Local social and political factions are sometimes intrusive into the elective process.

This writer's own preference is for an appointive board with appropriately staggered terms, designated by the governor of the state. However, there are potential problems with this system as well. Partisan political interests often become involved, and the president may find himself pulled toward involvement in gubernatorial campaigns. Caution is advised, of course. While appointive boards will indeed tend to bring to governance highly competent persons from the established area power structure, there may be some tendency to neglect representation from other constituent groups which are less organized in political affairs and in participation.

However selected, locally based boards tend to have some first-hand knowledge of the workings of the college. While members are more accessible to various internal and external constituencies and must guard against inappropriate responses, they are in the best position to exercise effective governance over college affairs.

The layering of a second board for junior colleges between the local board and the state coordinating board is both inefficient and unnecessary. Further, this is likely to exacerbate governance and administrative problems, add another layer of bureaucracy with associated controls, and increase non-instructional costs to the tax-payers. On the other hand, if no strong state coordinating board for all of higher education exists in the legal structure, then a state coordinating board for junior colleges with limited and carefully defined powers will likely benefit both the interests of the state and the colleges which are governed.

There is a need in each and every state for a strong state coordinating board with constitutional, rather than statutory, powers. This body should have powers which include estimating the needs and work loads of institutions, evaluating funding proposals, proposing the system's funding needs to the state's chief executive and legislative body, and dividing and distributing the funds which are appropriated according to a system set in policy or law. This is a much better arrangement than having each college going separately to the legislature to lobby for its needs in competition with others. This board should also have certain powers over degrees and credentials to protect against abuse and over academic articulation among institutions to assure the free movement and transfer of students without hardship.

It is important, however, that this coordinating board's powers be carefully defined and limited in constitutional law so that it does not presume to become a super-board of governance for all the colleges and universities in the state, nor is the legislature tempted to make it so by statute. It is well if the powers of institutional governing boards are also established within the constitution so as to prevent the drift toward state level infringement and centralization.

Conflicts in Governance

Usurpers of presidential power are legion. Each president must guard against allowing his limited powers to dissipate by default. Delegation of responsibility internally may relocate power, if such is sanctioned by board action or policy. Quite often student and faculty constituencies and/or their representatives and councils strive for increased powers guaranteed by board approval of organizational constitutions or by board policy. In the exercise of their policy making role and in the establishment of controls, sometimes over detail, governing boards may inadvertently be limiting the authority of their presidents.

Empire-building occurs at all levels, including the level of the state coordinating board, whether this be a board for junior colleges or for all of higher education. Presidents and local governing boards must be constantly alert for symptoms and signs of empire expansion at the state level. Too much is at stake to allow the vestiges of local autonomy to slip quietly away.

There are several influences or forces which militate toward increased power of the state coordinating board and its bureaucracy. Accountability is one of these. As state dollars become increasingly scarce, and difficult to extract through the political process, increased demands for accountability of institutions is made. While such exercises for assuring accountability quite often increase administrative costs and remove resources from active educational use, these are nevertheless constantly in demand.

Related to the above is the demand from legislators, the governor, and the state bureaucracy that control of the system be exercised from the top down, so that they can obtain definitive, quick answers and responses. News media often join in demanding quick action from the top for major or minor abuses, real or fictional, which they "expose" at individual institutions. This sets up a significant conflict not yet fully recognized by citizen and governance interests, whose flaming desire is to keep their institutions locally responsive. Since those in political power at the state capitol have the law-making power, they tend to win the struggle. As a result, there has been increasing state regulation, along with state mandates and dictates, and the authority over higher education has more often than not been assigned to state boards and executives of that board, or the non-educational state bureaucracy itself.

In summary, there has been an unhealthy shift in power from institutional governing boards to state coordinative boards and state executive department authorities. This shift in power further limits the autonomy of individual boards to govern and presidents to exercise creative leadership in their respective colleges and universities. It is imperative that such shifts, or sometimes "grabs," be recognized and brought into the open forum for discussion and evaluation. Presidents have an obligation to resist these efforts, and further obligations to inform governing boards and to assist in marshalling antagonist forces, when these changes threaten the future well-being of their educational operations. As Dr. J. A. Leone, former Oklahoma chancellor, said, "I am convinced that lay governance will never work smoothly, but I know of no better alternative."

Topics for Discussion or Further Study

1. Why is the official institutional structure typically not normally sufficient to provide ample opportunity for participation in college affairs? What can be done to improve its role in this regard?

2. Obtain a copy of a faculty organizational constitution or written policy description and do a formal analysis of this from the viewpoint of the president's office.

3. Obtain a copy to the description of an institution's faculty committee structure with role descriptions and analyze this for effectiveness and for problems.

4. Is it necessary that a college have an independent "faculty association" in order to meet internal governance expectations of external bodies such as accrediting associations? Generally, what would be the reasonable expectations of such groups?

5. Obtain the legal definition of powers for an institutional governing board and those for a coordinating board in the same state. Analyze these for overlap, conflict, degree of clarity, and the criteria mentioned in the text material. Provide case study material on the actual functioning of the system.

6. Write a two paragraph summary describing trends in governance in a state with which you are familiar, extrapolating these into the future from a college perspective.

FACETS OF
ADMINISTRATION

7

The writer recalls responding to a question from a governing board member during his interview for the presidency many years ago. The question called for a personal statement as to what this candidate perceived as his strong and weak points. The reply went something like this:

"I understand academics very well. I am familiar with collegiate curricula and curriculum development. I am knowledgeable about accreditation. I believe that I understand how faculty people think, and I can communicate with them. Coming from a counseling background, I think that I understand how to work with students and their needs. I am not an accountant, and I would have to learn about budgeting and finance. I am relatively unfamiliar with construction and with areas such as building maintenance. I would not consider myself to be strong in public relations, nor is that my area of greatest interest."

Considering the answer, it may be surprising that the respondent was selected to be a president. Such a candidate might not fare so well in today's competitive market. However, these remarks are not quoted for reasons of brilliance, or even to illustrate the type of candor believed to be desirable in the selection process, but these are given to illustrate some of the various facets of significance to successful administration of an institution.

Consider the various facets of college operations and the role of the president in these. First, some comments may be in order. Although the president is likely to have delegated managerial responsibility to others for operations within each of the areas discussed, he does not remain aloof to events and developments or the performance of the institution in all of these.

Not only does the president retain an active interest in each facet, but he exercises a leadership force throughout the institution. He must set the tone. He must assist in setting goals and objectives. He must observe and evaluate performance. And, he must intervene on occasion to prevent gross error and to redirect thrusts and efforts. The president is not, and must not become, sidelined by some simplistic philosophy regarding delegation. The president should not be overly sensitive to the feelings of subordinates about interference, although these must be taken into account in his approach to supervision.

Although open and candid discussions within the administrative team, and between the president and subordinates managing various facets, are appropriate and helpful, the president can not afford to have continuous, running debates with a subordinate who differs on the goals, philosophy, and style of administration in a particular area that area. While specialist administrators in each area should have decision making authority within defined limits, and each should be encouraged to use initiative in developing and implementing program ideas, it is imperative that these be exercised in a manner compatible with overall institutional goals, objectives, and administrative philosophy, which is the domain of the president.

PERSONNEL ADMINISTRATION

At one time, personnel administration was an area which seemed simple, and which tended to be handled somewhat intuitively in the regular course of routine, however, this has become an area of some complexity and thus a specialty within administration. Institutions tend to assign the procedural aspects of personnel administration to one particular office, although in small institutions this may be only one of several duties assigned to that administrator. Sometimes the president's executive secretary may be in charge, or perhaps an administrative assistant to the vice president of academics or business.

Personnel administration, as is focused upon here, is that area of procedural and record keeping functions rather than one of personnel relations. Matters pertaining to personnel management and personnel relations are discussed in Chapter 8.

Legal considerations have contributed to making this a sensitive area, and a strong commitment to the concepts of social justice has made it a very significant area. It is important that the person in charge of this office receive a very direct message from the president that it is to be operated in compliance with requirements, and that the institution is deeply concerned that opportunities for qualified members of under-represented groups be enhanced.

The president should be involved in employment decisions. In employment of faculty in smaller institutions, the president should join with the academic administrator and the division or department head in conducting a group interview. The president should be similarly involved in scanning the credentials of candidates considered to be better qualified and in the selection of interviewees. The president should be present and join the discussion of merits of candidates with his subordinates, and must approve the final selection regardless of the screening procedure utilized.

In smaller institutions the president should at least meet every person who is employed in support positions, for he will likely have some later contact with them and he must make the recommendation to the board. Board members are often more interested and more sensitive to the employment of local people in support positions than they are to the employment of professional staff whom they do not know or feel qualified to judge. In checking references for local people who may come from a neighboring town where there is a board member, it is often wise to include that board member in a check of reference individuals generally knowledgeable of the person. Sometimes such a check reveals problems which would be encountered in an embarrassing way during board consideration of an appointment. It should be noted that this is not, and should never become, a matter of patronage, but rather an informational check.

The foregoing discussion is not intended to imply that employment decisions are dominated by the president, but rather to sound cautions about becoming aloof to the process. Regardless of the particular participative system which is arranged within the college, the president must retain an active involvement and maintain some general control of the process. This is particularly true in smaller institutions in settings other than urban, but even in more complex environments the president should not allow his participation in such matters to slide away by default or in the negotiations process.

The discussion here has been in terms of general principles. Every institution is expected to have a broad spectrum of personnel policies and procedures covering almost every possible matter or occurrence. If such is not the case, then it becomes one of the first duties of the president to work with affected groups in developing a profile of policies for recommendation and inclusion in the board's policies and procedures manual.

The president must sometimes curtail the tendency of subordinates to engage in "top of the hat" situational management without proper reference to existing policy. The president himself must be cautious in this regard. While the writer is not advocating excessive rigidity or the overlooking of case considerations, following well conceived and clear policy directions is always the safest and best practice in administration.

The area of personnel administration, and its accompanying policies and procedures, is considered an extremely important one for presidents. For this reason, an entire chapter is devoted to the subject later in this book.

ACADEMICS

Although the college is filled with academic specialists, the president must not forget that he, too, is an academician by education and by experiential background. He must not become so preoccupied by other distractions in management that he neglects this most important sphere of operations within the institution. As indicated earlier, the president has an identity as faculty leader even though he delegates day to day administration, initiative, and problem resolution to others. It is important that the faculty views the president as vitally concerned with academic matters, although they tend to be quite sensitive to usurpation of their prerogatives in this area.

Curriculum initiatives in terms of course development and instructional methodology tend to come from within the academic sector. However, program initiatives, deletions, and new thrusts tend to come from the administration itself. Technological shifts in the instructional process may come from either sector.

It has long been noted that faculty are very difficult people to lead, and they are almost impossible to drive. It is true also that faculty are often negative toward administratively led innovations and changes. This may be frustrating, but it is not necessarily deleterious to the long term welfare of higher education.

Faculty have had great exposure to academic tradition, and they are usually very concerned about matters such as standards. This characteristic keeps faculty from being stampeded into following academic fads and superficial trends. Most faculty are willing to be experimental up to a point, but few are willing to be revolutionary. This will help the institution to avoid tangential errors in following fads, and will assist in maintaining a course of evolutionary change, rather than undergoing the turbulence of abruptness.

The president himself must be the number one guardian of academic standards. He must carefully evaluate changes in administrative procedure, calendar proposals, acceptance of experiential or nontraditional credits, introduction of new teaching technology, examination scheduling practices, office hour requirements, studies of grading practices, and a myriad of other routines and operations within the institution for effects upon the basic qualitative standards of the instructional program. Even those changes which may not be thought at first glance to have academic concomitants must be examined for ripple effects.

While faculty are expected to be the most concerned with instructional quality standards, administrators such as the president must also exercise constant vigilance. Because of their reputation as adaptable and resilient institutions, community and junior colleges may be particularly susceptible to fads which are touted to be on the "cutting edge" of the movement. While experimentalism may be advantageous in lesser degrees, it is not necessarily a safe practice as a general tone for the institution. Sometimes faculty, as well as instructional administrators, are caught up in the groundswell of untested and inadequately evaluated trends.

FINANCIAL AFFAIRS

With financial affairs, as is with other facets of administration, the best course of action for a president is to find a properly trained and experienced administrative specialist and charge him/her with responsibility for management of all financial affairs. This is not that simple. The writer has heard experienced presidents state that as long as the president controls the purse strings of the college he controls the important events within that institution. That, too, is an oversimplification.

It is of great importance that the president have a competent business officer. But, as with other matters, the president must remain involved in budget development and budget administration. The president must have necessary working knowledge of proper business office procedures, as defined by law, policy, and regulation. He must have at his fingertips, and in his mind, the essential facts of the college's financial condition. He must understand the sources of funding, and how these are derived. He must understand the process and procedures of budgeting and of purchasing. He must understand some of the general concerns and objectives of auditing, and must be able to interpret audit reports. While he does not work daily with detailed figures, he must develop sufficient knowledge that he can intuitively recognize gross errors and blunders.

The president and the business officer must be of one accord on the strategies of account management. They must be of one accord on other matters such as strict adherence to policy and legal prescriptions, retention in the files of all necessary documentation for clarity and audit trails, and conformity to business ethics and unquestioned honesty.

The president should be personally involved in all of the major purchases and business transactions of the college. Reference is made here to construction contracts, purchases of expensive equipment, site acquisitions, and business events of that general nature. It is important that he have first hand information about these matters, and that he has assurance that they are being properly handled.

The president should also be involved in business decisions that set a pattern or a theme throughout the college. Such an instance would be the choosing of a line or style of furnishings to be purchased for faculty offices or classrooms. It is well if a relationship is developed between the president and the business officer which has within it an understanding about matters appropriate for consultation, and matters which are considered routine intra-office management responsibilities.

Professionals with experience in several different colleges have probably encountered at least one petty tyrant in a business office, and perhaps one or more officious clerks. Students also encounter such people on occasion. The president should resolve that he will not tolerate such behavior within the institution he administers. The college business office is an important and a necessary service function, but it is not the focus of institutional life. It is important that personnel in that office understand the service role and the necessity for personal and professional courtesy in their relations with faculty, students, or other personnel.

Conversely, various campus constituencies often regard the business office as a necessary evil at best. Some would like to operate impet-uously and without the restraints that office places upon them. In such instances, the president and other members of the administrative team, as well as division chairs, must come together to persistently and patiently explain the limits within which the college's business affairs must be conducted, then insist upon conformity. Much depends upon the manner in which the business officer and his staff meet and deal with these other constituencies. Most staff will accept necessary constraints if presented courteously and with an explanation.

The president must receive regular, periodic reports on the status of all college accounts. Many prefer these to be monthly, although they may need to be received more often under certain conditions and at certain times of the fiscal year. Both the president and the board should receive a monthly status report on the budget, and its receipts and expenditures to date. The board has a fiduciary responsibility to ensure that the college is spending within the budgeted funds available.

It should be remembered, however, that reports require time and, for this reason, each report should have a purpose or be eliminated. Nevertheless, with the ubiquitous use of computers, there may be a tendency to generate unnecessary and unneeded reports. Too frequently these are in a format which is difficult to read and to distinguish the significant from the insignificant. The business office has an obligation to simplify its reporting.

As long as it employs auditors who check both the validity of the financial statements and compliance with policies and regulations, the board need not be involved in the business detail of the college. It is not necessary that the board review a list of purchases by vendor and amount each month, unless such is required by law. This level of micro-supervision is inappropriate, distracting, and produces additional logistical problems for the business office and the administration. A procedure involving approval of individual vendor claims delays payments and introduces a note of uncertainty with the business community.

It is important, however, for the board to be involved in an approval role with the major business transactions of the college. The board should review construction bids, purchase of real estate, and other purchases over some set sum (such as $5,000). The board should also approve the disposal of expensive property. Most public institutions must operate within some legal framework of restrictions. The president should be aware of these restrictions and should keep the board informed on such matters.

While it is important for the institutional business office and the president to have maximum latitude in the conduct of college business affairs within legal limitations, the president should also recognize the desirability of keeping the governing board informed of all significant developments and problems. When a crisis comes, an informed board can be helpful and supportive.

Further, while it is not desirable for the board by policy, or even consistent precedent, to be involved in the approval of decisions at certain levels, the president should be cognizant of the fact that board approval may be his best form of protection if controversy arises about some particular matter. The writer is not encouraging extreme caution, but simply suggesting that sensitive matters of any level be passed before the board for information (official record) or for approval.

One final word should be passed to presidents, business officers, and boards. This is in regard to auditors' reports. Auditors' reports are a fiduciary necessity and must be accepted as such. However, these reports and their management letters often get into areas which are subjective in nature. That is, these sometimes offer opinions or make directives based upon judgments and opinions.

Most audit suggestions are useful to institutional administrators, but this is not the case universally. Some audit suggestions may be unrealistic, contrary to the management goals of the administration, expensive to implement, or deleterious to the internal or external relationships of the institution. In such cases, the response of the administration should so state courteously, explaining why the college cannot or should not follow the suggestion.

It must be clear to all concerned that auditors are not employed to administer or manage the college. They are employed to check financial data, check documentation, certify the standing of college accounts, and to check compliance with policies, laws, and regulations. While most of their recommendations on internal control and procedural matters should be seriously studied, these must not be accepted as dictates without question or evaluation.

It should be understood also that in public colleges and universities, audits performed and reports issued by public officials or bureaucrats may or may not be completely valid or free of subjectivity. Auditors who work for an elected public official, or one who aspires to higher office, may be prone to overstatements, particularly when such reports are to be released to the media. Audits have been known to be used as political weapons when persons in the institution have angered someone in political power, or when there may be a desire to replace the president with someone politically more acceptable. Sometimes special audits are conducted as a result of complaints by a local faction or interest group and these type audits may be of a more severe nature.

All this is simply to suggest that audits are not sacrosanct. They are performed by people, most of whom are professionals with no underlying motives other than that of performing a duty of extreme significance to the institution. Auditors provide assurance of proper fiduciary responsibility. However, there are so many gray areas in fiscal activity, so many different rules and regulations, and so many different interpretations of these, that an overly officious or improperly motivated auditor can cause administrators anguish which may be unnecessary and undeserved.

STUDENT AFFAIRS

Although the president will see students and visit with them almost daily, personnel in the office of student affairs may be exceptionally helpful to him in keeping abreast of student interests and concerns. Research studies of this office, the registrar, and the institutional research and development office will keep him informed about changes and trends in the student clientele of the college. The president must be informed about special areas, such as student financial aid, and the problems being encountered there.

The division of student personnel is extremely important as an ancillary support service relevant to the academic mission of the college. Much has been said and written about the concept of the "whole" person, the significance of social and cultural growth to accompany academic development, the inhibitions of learning associated with social and emotional problems, and the significance of educational and career goal setting as the basis of student motivation.

Certainly the president must be familiar with the various facets of student personnel administration. He must understand the significance of accurate record keeping, confidentiality, and safe storage. He should recognize that streamlining the registration process will attract students and produce less frustration for them. He must understand the need for an active orientation program for first year students. He must have a general knowledge of student financial aids and the significance of these in extending equality of educational opportunity to all social and economic strata. He should understand the difference between academic advisement and student counseling and offer his support to both functions. He must understand the menace of drugs, alcohol, and sexually transmitted diseases to student welfare, and be supportive of special policies and programs to meet these threats. He must also be aware of the particular concerns of minority students.

The division of student services is a much more complex administrative area than is often supposed. It encompasses all of those areas mentioned above, and in addition others such as student activities, student housing, parking and traffic, security, and student discipline. It requires competent and credentialed personnel. Since student services produces no credit hours, which sometimes drive institutional budget formulae, there may be a tendency to view this division as less essential than it is. Services such as guidance and counseling are sometimes targeted when cuts become necessary. To cut these areas is a gross misjudgment in priorities.

It is unrealistic to attempt to discuss in any detail the management concerns relative to all of the facets of student personnel administration. Also, singling out specific areas may suggest that they are considered more significant than others. However, it may be worthwhile to give momentary mention to a few of these.

The need for counseling and guidance is generally understood, although their scope and complexity may not be. Drug and alcohol education and concerns with sexually transmitted diseases have added new educational dimensions to this service. Further, it is well if the president understands the function of this office which is seldom mentioned in the professional literature. This is the role of ombudsman. The president should lead counselors to accept and exercise the role of student ombudsman in assisting students with problems with faculty or other college offices and personnel. The president must also lead administrative and faculty personnel in accepting counseling staff as ombudsmen for student problem resolution. Note that an ombudsman is not necessarily an advocate, but he assists the student through the contacts necessary for problem resolution. Counselors and other student personnel staff do have an obligation for advocacy of student welfare interests in meetings with committees, planning councils, and the like.

Student discipline is ordinarily not a large problem for campuses without dormitories or other single student housing. Most campus discipline problems arise from the housing sector, or as a result of having those students on campus twenty-four hours a day and weekends. Student discipline may be quite time consuming on campuses with hundreds of students in residence. Also, residential campuses will require much more extensive student recreational and activities programs, and the facilities to accommodate these, as well as the budget to support personnel. Too frequently needs of residential campuses are ignored in state or other funding systems.

The athletic program is usually classified under the area of student activities, and thus the student affairs division. However, this is not always the case, and in some instances the president may want the athletic director to report directly to his office. Much depends upon the complexity of the program, and the personal characteristics of those charged with responsibility for that program and for the division. The athletic program is too delicate an area to leave under loose care and supervision. There are often considerable sums of money involved, and all too frequently there are irregularities which gain public attention or even notoriety. Support groups, while a blessing in many ways, can pose problems. It is well for the central administration to keep a watchful eye on matters pertaining to athletics, while offering support for an important sector of student and community life.

The question sometimes arises, particularly from the faculty constituency, as to whether intercollegiate athletics has values sufficient to offset the expenditures associated with it. There is no simple answer to this question. Perhaps one approach is to ask the same question regarding other student service functions, even about certain academic programs as well. Much of what transpires in educational institutions is difficult to justify except in terms of general human interest.

Rampant and expensive athletic programs in community and junior colleges are probably inappropriate, especially if they are operated under a budget which requires that sacrifices be made in academic related areas or if they detract from other necessary student personnel functions. Much of the seemingly required emphasis on athletic expenditures in junior colleges comes about in order to maintain competitiveness with like institutions. Scholarships tend to rise to the highest levels offered by competitors. While students should receive some scholarship recognition for the time they devote to training and representing the college, it is likely that with cooperation and proper regulation costs could be significantly reduced.

No discussion of student life and student activities can be complete without some mention of the significance of the fine arts at the collegiate level. Community colleges are considered to be the higher education institutions for the average citizen. They are also recognized for their contributions to career education, and for training and re-training of workers for business and industry. But the community college should be a complete institution, and it cannot be so without some stress on the humanities in its curriculum and on the fine arts in its activities program. The fine arts have never flourished without the benevolence of sponsors and benefactors.

The president of any collegiate institution must consider himself a patron or sponsor of fine arts activities and events on campus. He must set an example by his interest and by his attendance at events. He must also promote these activities with staff, students, and the general public. He must be willing to devote financial resources to assure quality instructional programs and quality performing arts activities on campus. If he fails to do so, the fine arts will languish, and students will be missing a significant component of their college experience.

FACILITIES

It is unfortunate that the primary gauges used by the public to evaluate the progress of the college and the success of the president are enrollment statistics and new campus buildings. They generalize that if enrollments are increasing then the college must be doing well. They point to the growth of the campus and its structures, and they grant credit to the work of the president. Some gauge the quality of the institution by the maintenance and cleanliness of the buildings. It is not necessary for the president to understand this thinking, nor is it necessary for him to accept it as valid, but it is wise if he accepts the reality of these perceptions and judgments.

Usually the supervision of maintenance of buildings and grounds falls under the direction of the college business officer, and this is appropriate. This is a function which cannot be neglected. The president must on occasion make inspections for himself, and he must relay those observations which are made casually in his circuits around the campus.

It is helpful if faculty division heads, and sometimes other administrators, are brought into the process. Each division chair should assume responsibility for reporting maintenance needs and custodial problems to the maintenance superintendent (or business office), and there should be an established procedure for doing so. Faculty should be encouraged to work through their chair in making needs known. The president should let it be known that after a maintenance item or problem has been reported twice, that the third report should come to his office.

The institution should have a long-range facilities plan, spanning three to five years ahead. Never should the college engage in expensive construction projects based upon what the president or anyone else in the college or on the board believes would be the "nice" thing to do at the moment. What is meant by this is that the need for new or remodeled buildings is one which develops and evolves, and such must be evaluated and reevaluated over a period of time.

Priorities change. It has been observed that a facility which was a "hot" item on the list one year sometimes failed to make the list a year or so later. A building program cannot be based on a whim, even if the whim is the president's. There is a need for long-range planning, continuing discussions, accumulating statistics, setting and rearranging of priorities, and all the other processes important to solid planning efforts for the future. Buildings and facilities last for years, therefore it behooves the institution to devote time to planning and priority-setting. This is not an area for impetuousness, but one for patience.

It is beneficial if the college has a continuing business relationship with a single architectural and engineering firm, providing that such contacts and services have been satisfactory in the past. Such an arrangement allows the firm to become totally familiar with the campus topography and underground services, as well as its structures and heavy equipment in place. The firm can carry out themes over a period of time, and its specifications may include equipment with interchangeable parts with existing machinery. Of some importance, under this continuing relationship a firm will often assist with planning efforts, campus master plans, and illustrations free of charge.

PUBLIC RELATIONS

Public relations is indeed an area of significance, but it is not at the level of significance that many place upon this facet of administration. As an example, it is important for the president to be known in the community, but it is more important for him to be respected.

Generally speaking, if a president develops a quality institution offering quality academic and other services to its clientele, then public relations will tend to take care of themselves. Of course, the remaining task is one of informing the public about what is transpiring within the college, for the bloom of the college must not blush unseen.

There are several ways of informing the public. Probably the best way is by word-of-mouth on the part of students being served. The second best way is through the utilization of media of all kinds. The speaking efforts of the president and the staff, and the personal contact efforts of the president, probably rank a poor third and fourth. Nevertheless, these efforts should not be neglected.

It is important that the college have a person who specializes in the public information function. Such an office will see that news releases are provided to local newspapers and radio or television stations regularly, and that these tell the stories of the college in a positive way. This individual should be considered a part of the administrative team, and the president should be able to count on loyalty and support from this sector. This is not a pure journalistic function, but a public relations effort. This person may assist or manage the college's marketing efforts as well, providing printed and other materials for use in that thrust.

While some of the above comments may appear to downplay the president's community contact activities, the purpose of these remarks is to place this activity in proper perspective. Often board members and others are anxious for the president to be seen a lot in public and to be involved with every community project. Too often presidents misplace their priorities allotting too much time to this aspect of their duties, therefore neglecting those which are more significant to the institution's health. Some presidents find satisfaction in their off-campus contacts as compensation for their frustrations on campus. For whatever reasons, the public relations function should not be given priority beyond its worth to the welfare of the college.

Perhaps a word is in order about political relations. This is, of course, a very delicate area. The president must be actively involved in political relations but not in politics. The president should be considered politically neutral as far as partisanship. He should also maintain a neutrality in board elections if his board is chosen in that manner. This does not mean that the president cannot maneuver in the political arena and among politicians. In a public college, especially one which is state supported, it is essential to the institution that the president establish and maintain a good rapport with key elected officials.

Just as the president maintains an arms-length distance from active participation in elective politics, he must also expect that those in the political arena will maintain an arms-length relationship with the institution. That is, elected officials, and especially legislators, may be expected to support the needs of the institution as a constituent agency but not to regard it as a political fiefdom. Boards can often assist the president in serving as a buffer from political patronage efforts should such come about.

Topics for Discussion or Further Study

1. It is said that the president sets the "tone" for an institution. In what ways does he do this?

2. How can the president be involved in personnel decisions without dominating the process?

3. Equal opportunity is paramount in the personnel selection process. From experience and from readings, what are the accepted procedures to ensure equal opportunity? How do attitudinal and more subtle considerations enter the scene? What is the president's obligation in this area?

4. Why must special attention be given by the president to athletics as only one facet of the student activities program? What are some of the inherent dangers in this area?

5. How, or in what ways, do the president's posture, communications, and actions affect the college's academic standards?

6. Are presidents traditionally perceived by faculty as favoring high academic standards? Why? Why not?

7. Why must the president keep a careful watch on the business affairs of the college?

8. Is there a danger that presidents may become too involved with public relations? Why would this be a problem?

PERSONNEL POLICIES
AND PRACTICES

8

INTRODUCTION

Personnel administration in community colleges has become an area of extreme complexity. Larger institutions now have offices and administrators with special expertise in this area, but smaller colleges must continue to rely upon the general knowledge of the president and his supporting cast in the academic and business sectors. In another context this writer has said:

> This has become an area laden with pitfalls and potential controversy which may involve liabilities in resources, risks to professional careers, and threats to institutional reputations. It is, nevertheless, the window of opportunity for the college leader who seeks to make substantive changes and improvements in the most basic of services related to the institutional mission.
>
> (Vineyard in Cohen and Brawer, 1993)

There is indeed no endeavor more significant to building excellence into an academic institution than the procurement, development, and retention of quality, professional personnel. The mission of the community college is one of instruction and human service. Those who carry out these significant functions must be selected with care and provided with the supportive and enhancing environment which will afford opportunities for professional growth, as well as service to the clientele.

The material which follows leans toward the mainstream approach. That is to say, the ideas and suggestions contained herein may be more applicable to the thousand or so small and medium junior colleges than to the larger, urban institutions, which probably have expertise in the form of personnel offices and directors. Further, it is to be understood that the existence of collective bargaining situations, or other structures and conditions, may make some suggestions inapplicable. In some states there are statutes which govern certain areas of personnel relationships and practices, and these must be taken into account. Participative governance systems established within an institution may negate applicability of some methodologies. The assumption of *collegiality* is inherent in many recommended procedures.

Further, legal considerations loom as a significant aspect of personnel administration. These include both enacted and case law. While suggestions will be made in conformity with a layman's understanding of the law, and citations of case law may be made, these are not intended as the offering of legal advice. Neither is it intended here to lure the uninitiated into the fallacies of acting as one's own lawyer in situations where legal counsel is appropriate and needed. At times the president's best friend may well be the college's legal advisor.

RECRUITMENT OF PROFESSIONAL STAFF

Academic Credentials

During the last decade or so, there has been considerable discussion, and some debate, as to the appropriate credentials for community college faculty. Some traditionalists hold to the view that the master of science or master of arts degrees are the only appropriate academic preparation for college teaching, including the junior college. Those academic administrators in smaller two-year colleges, who have had to struggle with problems of fitting instructor qualifications to a diversified class schedule, have espoused the notion that broad field preparation, versus the narrow discipline approach, is much more appropriate. Some have advanced the idea that the properly prepared community college instructor, in addition to academic preparation, should have some work in professional areas, such as community college philosophy and curriculum, psychology of both the young and mature adult, measurements, the learning process, and perhaps measurements and statistics. Most university programs designed to prepare community college personnel have taken the latter approach.

The significance of graduate degrees is sometimes debated. A few have voiced negative views of the doctoral degree, particularly the Ph.D., for junior college teaching. Most still value the doctoral degree, however. The master's degree has been commonly accepted as the base credential for junior colleges. It is not unusual in technical or occupational programs to find persons teaching with a baccalaureate credential, or sometimes with only the associate degree, in some highly specialized program where staff with academic education are extremely scarce. Nevertheless, the institution which prides itself on its standards will press staff lacking the master's degree toward that objective, possibly providing some financial assistance.

Instructional experience is quite important in the search for new teaching staff. For many years the secondary school system was the principal recruiting ground for community college staff, and it is still fertile ground for competent instructors who are ready to move to a new level of teaching. Now, many institutions look more to universities for academic staff in the transfer curricular areas. Finding qualified candidates with teaching experience other than as a graduate assistant is rare from that source.

The recruitment of practicing professionals from the private arena has become more common. For some time it has been popular to recruit evening class instructors from the business world as adjunct personnel. With the advent of the early retirement options in the private sector, a new pool of qualified and experienced personnel has been opened to the community college. Similarly, the pool coming from early military retirement is a rich resource of academically competent, mature individuals, some with instructional experience. It should be noted that teaching accounting to a group of college students may be vastly different from the sophisticated world of corporate commerce. Many an evening class dean, and unfortunate evening class students, have found this to be true.

In order to attract and retain persons with relevant experience as well as those with advanced degrees, salary schedules must provide incentives. These must retain a proper balance, however, so the proportions of the college's salary budget are directed fairly. It has been noted that a few institutions have so weighted experience credits in their schedules as to force beginning salaries below an academic "poverty" norm. Further, some schedules limit severely the experience credits available to faculty coming into the college, regardless of actual experience. This usually comes from a weighty influence of experienced faculty in negotiating processes. Whatever the source, such practices are deleterious to the building of a strong academic faculty corps.

Recruitment Procedures

Faculty and professional staff recruitment begins with a properly written definition of the position or assignment. This is translated into descriptions of the position for the purposes of advertisement and/or circulation. The advertisement may be more succinctly phrased than the circularized version, but both may be summarizations of a lengthier definition of responsibilities. Descriptions for administrative positions are usually more lengthy than those for faculty.

Usually position or assignment descriptions originate with the division head or the academic dean (vice president), although personnel offices (where such exist) will assist with their refinement. This task should not be taken lightly. The wording of this description, and the requirements and preferences desired in its applicants may be very significant in the case of a legal challenge. The institution can become vulnerable if it deviates from its own announcement specifications. The assignment and the qualifications expected should, of course, have a justifiable relationship.

A single office is normally responsible for advertising vacancies and the receipt of applications for academic vacancies. Usually the office of the chief academic officer handles these duties, but it may become the responsibility of the office of the president. In either case it is important that office personnel be trained in proper procedures.

In meeting the requirements and the goals of equal opportunity and affirmative action, it is important that positions be advertised and circularized in such a fashion that groups under-represented in higher education will have every opportunity to become aware of the vacancy and thus become a part of the applicant pool. Some may overreact to these concerns by advertising all positions in national higher education publications. This may not be cost effective. However, top administrative posts should have national advertisement.

Again, an important consideration in faculty recruitment is the enlargement of the applicant pool to include under-represented groups. This may mean circularizing the placement offices and departments of institutions with heavy minority student populations even though these do not have graduate programs. It may mean advertisement in publications with circulation to minorities. Some colleges have developed special strategies which are useful. One rural college has a cooperative urban counterpart which mails its circulars to minority persons who are listed in its files. One college maintains a follow-up program of minority graduates geared toward recruiting among those who achieve advanced degrees.

Most junior colleges circularize vacancy announcements for both placement offices and academic departments of universities within a geographic region. Some also send these to the department offering professional courses in higher education and the junior college. Some send circulars to other community colleges in surrounding states. What is contained in these circulars? The contents may be summarized as follows:

Institution and location
Announcement date
Position title
Definition of assignment
Qualifications required and preferred
Length of contract period
Salary or salary range
Starting date for employment
Form of application
Closing date
Point of contact
Equal opportunity/affirmative action statement

Procedures may vary somewhat when searching for an instructor in a technical or occupational area. In this case, trade publications and newspapers with general circulation may be much more appropriate than those related to higher education. In general, colleges must adapt strategies to be in accordance with the position vacancy.

A word is in order regarding the use of application forms. If the college uses an application form, the wording of questions is extremely significant, as well as the inclusion or exclusion of certain questions from a legal point of view. All such forms should be examined by an attorney who is well versed in employment law. For these and similar reasons, most colleges rely upon the resume' prepared and furnished by the applicant rather than an application. Resumes provide the necessary information, and their use for application purposes assists in avoiding complications. Similarly, no pictures should be solicited with resumes. If the college wants such information to be placed in a personnel file to be created for the employed person, a basic personnel form for use with new hires is appropriate.

SELECTION OF STAFF

Screening

There should be one central collection point for application materials in a designated administrative office. This office should create a search file for every vacancy and retain this for at least five years. This file should contain copies of circulars, advertisements, and initialed notations of the circulation procedure. It will contain memos to file on all screening and selection actions taken. It will contain all resumes and correspondence. Standard check sheets with space for notations may be employed. The file will contain memos with an explanatory rationale for selections made as well as a complete record of all actions in connection with the vacancy. It should provide an audit trail for future examinations by an appropriate authority, and it provides documentation for the college in the case of challenge on legally protected grounds. Attention to propriety to this degree of detail may also increase sensitivity to fairness in the selection process.

In colleges with personnel offices, screening will be handled there. It is important to note, however, that the role of the personnel office is one of expedition and record keeping. It is not traditionally involved in the selection process itself. The personnel office may, however, be involved in screening applicants to the extent that it may separate those who meet advertised qualifications from those who do not.

Screening is that subjective process of examining of the paper material furnished by applicants to separate a smaller group of semi-finalists who should receive closer scrutiny. Once this is done, the process of choosing interviewees and deciding among them becomes one of *selection*. Normally, reference letters are neither solicited nor submitted with resumes from applicants. These come into play in the selection process rather than in the screening process.

Systems for screening and selection vary from college to college depending on their size. In some larger colleges, both screening and selection are done at the division or departmental level and involve the head and a staff committee. In other situations, the academic dean (vice president) may conduct the screening with the assistance of the division chairperson, and perhaps other staff, in the process. In some smaller colleges, the academic dean, the president, and the division head may constitute a screening "committee." Some colleges have a personnel committee which conducts screening and other procedures. While it is risky to choose among screening systems, within the small and medium sized colleges the lead of the chief academic officer and the involvement of the division and/or department chair as a screening team seem most appropriate.

Some presidents choose to remain aloof to both the screening and the selection processes. While this may be appropriate in the case of screening, it is highly questionable in the case of selection. It would, of course, be difficult for the president of a large urban college to be directly involved in this process. However, he should meet the interviewing finalists. The president must retain, and exercise when appropriate, his right of refusal of personnel recommendations. This is too important a process to let pass by default.

It is imperative that the institution have definite policies and procedures governing screening and selection processes. These should be clearly stated and simple to follow. The development of such policies forces colleges to examine critically and to clarify these procedures. Careful adherence in the execution of policies not only protects the institution but also produces greater fairness in the treatment of applicants.

The Selection Phase

The screening process results in a pool of more promising candidates, who might be termed semi-finalists. As a rule, references (in the form of letters) are not furnished by candidates. Instead each candidate supplies a list of names, addresses, and telephone numbers is supplied. When the field of candidates has been narrowed to a few, it is time to check references. To attempt to do so earlier in the screening process would be quite cumbersome and time consuming. Further, it is not fair to candidates who are not receiving serious consideration to have their current employment rapport disturbed, as sometimes happens. Although most candidates may have properly notified their references, it is well to notify these semi-finalists of their status and indicate that references are being contacted.

While reference letters are useful, those who give references have become very cautious about putting negatives in these. Telephone or personal contacts are considered more reliable. In the past, one person on the committee, usually the ranking member such as the dean, have taken on the responsibility of making telephone calls and keeping notes on these. With the advent of the speaker phone and easy conference calling, the entire committee may participate in this process. Questions may be scripted and shared, and each committee member hears the answers. Further, the committee may wish to contact persons other than the listed references since the views obtained from these are predisposed toward the positive. This can be done simply by title or a designation such as "a mathematics instructor" given to the switchboard operator at the candidate's college.

After consideration of references, the next step is selection of candidates for interviewing. There is no magic number. In some instances, one candidate may appear clearly superior to others. If so, then the one candidate should be interviewed and selected if found to be as good as appearances indicate. Some committees arrange top candidates into an hierarchy, interviewing them in an agreed upon order until satisfied. Some choose the top two or three. Interviewing can be a time consuming process, so the more efficient the procedure the better, as long as fairness and openness are practiced. It might also be mentioned that agreement on a selection may become more difficult as interview numbers increase.

The interviewing phase is an extremely important part of the selection process. It is usually better if the committee members interview each candidate as a group, rather than having individual interviews. This is less wearisome for the candidates, and offers opportunity for some scripting and sharing of questions as well as the advantage of common exposure for committee members.

Occasionally, committees decide to develop selection criteria for use in both screening and interviewing. This may add structure and fairness to the process, however, caution must be observed that the selection criteria does not impose additional "requirements" to the position that were not covered in the vacancy announcement.

The constituting of interview committees poses the same problems as mentioned in connection with screening. Normally, the screening group acts as the selection and interview committee. However, other persons may be added. Certainly, if the screening group is a general personnel committee, then persons from the area, including the chairperson, should be added. If the screening committee is made up of titular academic leaders such as the academic officer and department head, then at least one additional person from the field might be added. In smaller colleges the president may become a part of the interviewing and selection committee. Certainly, a brief office visit with titular leaders is always appropriate. It is well if the candidate meets other faculty persons in the field who are not on the committee. While these faculty members may not participate in formal deliberations, their input is often helpful.

Goals of the interviewing process include opportunities to obtain responses and form judgments about teaching and evaluation approaches, attitudes toward the student clientele served, willingness to make time commitments, congruence of individual and institutional philosophies, adaptability to the college and community environment, views on working relationships, institutional service outside the classroom, career ambitions, oral communicative skills, personality and mannerisms, and other relevant nuances.

During the interview, opportunity is also afforded for a brief orientation of the candidate to the internal systems of the college and expectations of the position according to college policies and practices. There is an obligation to present the college candidly as it is, so that the candidate may accept or decline employment from at least a modicum of needed information. Accepting employment under these honest conditions imposes some sense of obligation upon the new person.

Once the interviewing is done, how is the selection made? Much depends upon the selection structure employed, of course. One suggestion is generally applicable, and that is a search for consensus. Voting should be a formality undertaken after consensus is reached. If the committee is a departmental one, perhaps under the chair, then the committee makes a recommendation which the chair can support and this is taken up the academic chain and on to the president. It is important that there be an understanding in policy that there must be concurrence at each link in the chain, and that the matter could be referred back for further consideration and a new recommendation. Perhaps it is a bit more delicate when the president or the chief academic officer participates as a member of the committee. Nevertheless, the principle is the same. This is that the recommendation must be one which each titular leader can support even though it might not be the person most favored. No considerate dean or president desires to select a candidate who is unacceptable to the division chair, and the same courtesies should be returned.

In an institution which is characterized by a high degree of cohesiveness among professional staff, both faculty and administrative, and professional courtesies are a part of its interactive style, judgments tend to be similar and reaching a consensus is rarely a problem in assessing job candidates. On the other hand, an institution beset by competing faculty factions, friction and contention between faculty and administration, and fragmented by devotees of diverse instructional systems and institutional goals and philosophies, the selection process may become a battleground for these hostile and competing forces and no mutually participatory system for screening and selection of new staff will work well.

When confronted with such circumstances, presidents and other administrative leaders must resist any temptations to abdicate their responsibilities by giving this process over entirely to the faculty. The result of such a move may strengthen some faction's ability to advance its own agenda and goals for the college over those of others. Presidents who have a vision for the institution must view the faculty selection process as an important medium toward that vision. It is only through the work of the professional corps that goals are achieved, visions are fulfilled, and dreams are realized for the college.

PERSONNEL POLICIES

Need for a Policy System

A personnel policy system regulates, but it also protects. Without becoming excessively rigid, the institution needs a comprehensive set of personnel policies defining its relations with its professional staff and other employees. These policies serve to define the professional environment and conditions of service for staff. They regulate the inner dynamics of the institution. Kaiser and Greer (1988) discuss the various entanglements of a legal nature of personnel policies and practices.

What are some of the areas which a comprehensive set of personnel policies should include? The following list suggests topics which such policies may cover:

> *Equal opportunity and affirmative action*
> *Employment processes and procedures*
> *Role definitions and position descriptions*
> *Leaves and absences*
> *Tenure and dismissal*
> *Guidelines for workloads and assignments*
> *Fringe benefits*
> *Evaluation principles and system*
> *Retirement*
> *Academic freedom*
> *Professional development and improvement*
> *Extra-institutional commitments (outside work)*
> *Interpersonal relations (including sexual harassment)*
> *Institutional professional participative system*
>   *(internal governance; committee system; etc.)*
> *Retrenchment of staff*
> *Grievances*
> *Time and office obligations*
> *Vacations*
> *Internal communications channels*
> *Special areas*
>   *Drug-free workplace*
>   *Political actions and freedoms*
>   *Extensions of protected rights*
>   *(sexual orientation; etc.)*

The list above is not exhaustive, of course, but the range of topics is indicative of the complexity of a comprehensive set of personnel policies. It is important that policies define the expectations for administrators and for support staff, as well as faculty, and establish the rights reserved for each. Many will be the same, but some will be different.

While all of the above areas merit further discussion, limits of time and space dictate that only certain more significant ones be selected for further treatment in the sections which follow.

Professional Development

In earlier sections, the importance of recruitment and the selection process was stressed in bringing to the college fresh, bright, energetic professionals dedicated to the common goals and mission of the institution. Of equal importance is what happens to this group after it is assembled. Good colleges with able staff have been observed to stagnate. Others with similar human resources have been observed to go off on tangential courses, wasting energies on matters unrelated to the essential mission of the institution. Ideally, leadership should stimulate progress, which is change in the direction of carefully considered college goals while avoiding the former and latter mentioned pitfalls.

Professional development occurs as a result of group processes and individual experiences of stimulation. Individual experiences may be less flashy than group "programs," but these can be just as substantive in final effects.

Typically, in thinking of professional development programs, state meetings, regional conferences of disciplinary associations, national conventions, and sabbatical leaves come to mind. Seminars and workshops might be added.

The "in-house" workshop or seminar has become popular in recent years, and indeed these may be highly profitable for staff and the institution. Much depends upon the "readiness" of the staff for the particular experience and whether it meets a need of most of the individuals in the group. When only a few are interested, or when the topic is relevant for only a few, sending these to an outside event may be more cost and time-effective. Some colleges have gone so far as offering university graduate courses to staff on campus tuition-free. Such offerings may include courses dealing with a topic of common interest such as teaching technologies or educational measurements and assessments. One college actually offered a course on the American junior college on its campus for a faculty heavily steeped in university liberal arts traditions.

Some institutions go beyond the ordinary in offering professional development opportunities for staff. These may offer grants to faculty for classroom research projects or for those who are willing to work on special tasks related to the improvement of instruction. For example, a couple of English faculty members may be offered summer grants to develop videotapes for the English tutorial laboratory addressing common remedial needs of students. A science instructor may receive a grant to videotape science laboratory experiments as a learning resource for the library.

In 1982, Northern Oklahoma College approached the concept of sabbatical leave in a new and different fashion. This innovative program was termed Renewal and Revitalization, but affectionately known among faculty as "R and R." It provided financial assistance to professional staff who wanted to improve or to broaden their academic credentials through summer or part-time study. It covered expenses to attend special workshops or seminars (as contrasted with meetings or conventions provided for in the regular travel budget). Even broader in its scope, the program provided for personal travel experiences relevant to assignments. Thus, an English teacher might take a tour of Great Britain, or a history instructor might make a tour of Civil War battlefields. An instructor, or an administrator, might go for a site visit to another college which had achieved distinction for an exemplary program in some academic or administrative area.

The existence of such a program boosts spirits and offers opportunities for academic development. Presidents should not be reluctant to think freely in exploring new ideas for providing professional growth opportunities for institutional colleagues.

Faculty Compensation

Surveys of faculty compensation are legion. While this is an area of great importance to professional staff, psychological and social factors are probably even more important to faculty morale. Some of the more significant aspects of compensation for faculty tend to revolve around: (1) the fairness of compensation levels for the profession in relation to its value and position in the larger society; (2) compensation levels compared with other tiers in education, peer institutions, and individual peers within the institution; (3) the perceived fairness of methods utilized to arrive at compensation levels; and (4) the priority given to faculty compensation compared with other sectors of the college budget.

The most popular form of faculty compensation is often a salary schedule based upon degrees and experience. The popularity of this type of schedule can be attributed to a number of reasons, some of which include: (1) this is the simplest and most easily understood method; (2) when faculty have a voice through negotiations or internal governance input, these schedules are objective and thus protective against favoritism; (3) mutual distrust, bickering, and criticism among peers and between faculty and administration is minimized; and (4) failure of constituencies and peers to agree upon or to trust any system of judging merit.

Relatively few college leaders will attempt a compensation system which deviates far from the norm of the salary schedule based upon degrees and increments of experience. Even fewer venture to devise a compensation system with merit features "above the table." In spite of these hazards, a unique salary system involving merit ratings came into being at Northern Oklahoma College by vote of the faculty in 1967, and continues as the present-day system with some modifications. This innovative system is described in the inset which follows.

A Unique Salary System

This system combines credentials, experience, and merit components into a single algebraic index. It uses as a base an algebraic "X," an unknown variable set each year after the funds available to support the college budget become known. This "X" represents the salary of a master's degree person with no relevant experience credits. Increments in decimals are added to "X" for credentials above the master's level and for years of experience. Merit ratings are in increments of "X" based upon annual evaluation in three areas: Teaching performance, institutional service, and community involvement. Further increments may be made for service as a division chairperson, extra months obligation, or similar reasons. Reductions are made for credentials below the master's degree.

The outcome of the above is an "X-factor" for each member of the instructional staff. These tend to vary from about 1.15 to 1.55. Once the monetary value of "X" has been set, depending on the fiscal fortunes of the state and the college, each "X-factor" is multiplied by that value to determine individual salaries. Faculty will know their "X-factor" in the spring after evaluations, and thus their share in prosperity, even though the college budget and actual salaries may not be determined until summer. The college administration has the advantage of knowing the cumulative total of all "X-factors" in advance, and once the amount of money which can be devoted to salaries is determined, the process is one of arithmetic (or algebra) by first dividing to determine the value of the algebraic "X," then multiplying that by each individual's "X-factor to make a salary listing.

An individual faculty member's "X-factor" and salary calculation might appear as follows:

$1.00X$ *master's degree*
$.02X$ *15 credit hours additional graduate credit*
$.12X$ *first 4 years teaching experience*
$.06X$ *next 6 years teaching experience*
$.09X$ *instructional performance rating*
$.04X$ *institutional service rating*
$.02X$ *community involvement rating*
$1.35X$ *X-factor*
(Thus, if "X" is set at $26,000, then the salary is $35,100.)

Although there are other features to the system, it remains fairly simple in operation. It is understood that such a system, which provides for merit ratings done by the division chairperson and academic dean with review by the president, would not be acceptable in some college environments. Nevertheless, there are increasing pressures from public sector governance entities for salary systems which reward merit. Therefore, it behooves college leaders to search for systems which are acceptable both to academicians and the public's representatives.

EVALUATION OF FACULTY

A Rationale and an Instrument

Any evaluation system for judging faculty performance, or that of any other professional staff, should be based upon a rationale. The best beginning is a clearly stated definition of role expectations for the position. When properly conceptualized and properly phrased, such statements tend to evolve logically into an evaluation instrument. It is well, of course, if these statements of role expectation are developed through internal participative involvement in order to increase their acceptability.

The following inset showcases a rather comprehensive faculty role description. The origins of these ideas are unknown.

Faculty Role Description

1. *Demonstrates an understanding and support for the philosophy and mission of the community college.*
    A. *Understands transfer, career, and community service programs.*
    B. *Accepts the "student centered" concept.*
    C. *Explains well the role and purposes of the community college to others.*

2. *Demonstrates knowledge of subject matter.*
    A. *Exceptional preparation in the teaching area.*
    B. *Familiarity with research and current developments.*
    C. *Maintains respect of colleagues in the field.*

3. *Demonstrates understanding of the basic elements of the instructional process.*
    A. *Prepares and follows instructional objectives.*
    B. *Develops a variety of instructional strategies.*
    C. *Prepares criterion tests based upon objectives.*

    D. *Places priority on instruction duties as opposed to either personal or other professional interests.*

4. *Demonstrates the ability to communicate subject matter to students.*
   A. *Uses various methods, techniques, and materials to stimulate student mastery.*
   B. *Selects appropriate teaching materials and devices.*
   C. *Maintains the respect of students.*
   D. *Makes the knowledge relevant to students.*

5. *Demonstrates that instructional activities are well planned and congruent with catalog descriptions, syllabi, and course outlines.*
   A. *Prepares course and class session objectives.*
   B. *Develops instructional approaches fitted to a wide range of student abilities and backgrounds.*
   C. *Prepares before the course begins and for each class session.*
   D. *Plans special activities to complement formal instruction.*
   E. *Plans and conducts the course for continuity with others.*

6. *Understands and provides for individual differences.*
   A. *Utilizes instructional media.*
   B. *Encourages the use of available learning facilities.*
   C. *Adjusts outside work to the demands of the course.*
   D. *Assures that assignments are within the general competency level of students.*
   E. *Varies assignments and projects each term.*
   F. *Takes the role of advisor to students seriously.*
   G. *Is available to students outside of class.*

7. *Stimulates students to be active learners.*
   A. *Uses techniques appropriate to the material.*
   B. *Challenges students to set realistic goals.*
   C. *Relates new concepts to previous learning.*
   D. *Conducts classes in a manner conducive to enthusiasm and excitement.*
   E. *Encourages participation of all students.*

8. *Demonstrates the ability to judge student performance properly.*
   A. *Explains orally and provides a syllabus describing how grades are to be derived.*
   B. *Informs students regularly of their progress.*
   C. *Evaluates students according to reasonable standards.*
   D. *Develops and uses tests related to objectives.*
   E. *Uses written assignments and projects in evaluation.*
   F. *Uses tests as a learning experience.*
   G. *Hands back test results and exercises promptly.*

9. *Furnishes evidence of professional growth and development.*
   A. *Participates in activities related to the field.*
   B. *Participates in activities related to improvement of instruction and college service.*
   C. *Enrolls for credit, travels, and/or participates in faculty development programs.*
   D. *Welcomes constructive suggestions for improvement.*
   E. *Utilizes appropriate channels of communication.*
   F. *Assumes additional responsibilities as needed in institutional service.*
   G. *Participates in appropriate student organizations and student life.*

10. *Displays personal characteristics which reflect positively on the academic profession and upon the college.*
    A. *Respects colleagues, and observes ethical principles.*
    B. *Participates in contributory community organizations and activities.*
    C. *Demonstrates positive interaction with supervisors, colleagues, and support personnel.*
    D. *Uses an appropriate vocabulary free of profanity and excessive slang.*
    E. *Displays tact, discretion, and good judgment when meeting unusual or delicate situations.*
    F. *Recognizes the responsibility to the profession and the institution to present a favorable personal appearance in the classroom and at other college functions.*
    G. *Presents a generally positive view of the college.*
    H. *Fulfills time obligations and commitments.*
    I. *Avoids entangling the college unnecessarily in personal affairs or personal business.*
    J. *Uses judgment and restraint in exercising freedoms and privileges, and avoids entangling the college in issues irrelevant to its instructional mission.*

It is easy to see that a statement of role expectations such as the above may be readily adapted to provide an evaluation instrument. It is as simple as adding response categories such as "Usually," "Sometimes," "Seldom," and "Never" to the right in a check sheet format. Further, it will be noted that the statement is in *behavioral* terms. That is, it describes observable behaviors or indications which may be inferred from observations. In the past, the most common form of rating categories were on personal characteristics such as "attitude" or "professionalism." Adverse judgments made of these characteristics tended to be demeaning to the individual as a *person*. Critiques of behavior tend to be less damaging in their nature, and therefore more acceptable and more useful.

When faculty evaluation instruments are developed without the advantage of such a clear statement of expectations imbedded in policy, then these instruments themselves tend to define expectations and policy. In such instances, it is important that the evaluation instrument be a comprehensive one, since the results of the process are often used in making decisions affecting the future career of staff members. Further, since the college may possibly be in a position of defending its actions in the legal arena, it behooves the president to take an interest in the evaluation system and its instrumental criteria.

Seldin (1988) provides a rich source of material and formats for evaluation of professional staff. This is a valuable resource for those studying or planning evaluation systems.

Evaluation Procedures

There is, of course, much more to the evaluation process than the development of an instrument based upon institutional expectations. While this may be the more difficult task in an academic sense, establishing procedures for evaluation may be much more demanding in terms of consensus within the college. The big question becomes: "Who does the evaluating?"

Normally, there are strong objections to every possible suggestion on the evaluation process. Faculty tend to be suspicious of administrative evaluations and are reluctant to submit themselves to judgments from that sector. However, faculty may be even more reluctant to submit to the evaluations of peers within or outside of their department, especially if these involve competitive merit ratings or salary concomitants. Most are reluctant to engage in popularity contests in front of their students. For these and other reasons, it is important that proposed systems be submitted to the participative process and consensus sought.

Nevertheless, an evaluation system must not become so innocuous as to lose its effectiveness for personnel administrative purposes. It should be strong enough to support the tough decisions which must be made in certain cases within the personnel arena. Faculty are very hesitant to become a party to peer evaluations which involve, or lead toward, the decision for termination of a colleague. Student evaluations cannot be trusted for such purposes since students have a limited perspective from which to judge and their ratings tend to be influenced by academic work demands and grades expected. Systems which attempt to combine the above with weightings become so cumbersome, they are prone to collapse from their own "weights."

Therefore, truly effective and useful evaluation systems, as viewed from an administrative perspective, are usually authority based.

Much depends upon the professional rapport and the acceptance of structured relationships within the institution. In *collegial* situations, the evaluative process might well begin with the individual faculty member doing a self-evaluation and the department (or division) chair doing an evaluation, each utilizing the institutionally adopted instrument. This is followed by an interactive conference in which there is a sharing of views and perhaps some professional counseling, that will possibly lead to the alteration of one or both formalized sets of views. The next step is a three-way conference with the appropriate dean. After this conference, the dean prepares an evaluation form with a memorandum and his recommendations, if any, attached. This process moves upward throughout the review and approval process of titular leaders, perhaps moving as far up as the president. If merit ratings are involved, these are also recommended and attached by the dean after conferring with the division chair. These become a part of the personnel file, usually located in the office of the chief academic officer.

While the process described above is authority centered, something akin to this ordinarily proves to be the best for college administrative purposes, which include the culling of non-performers from the faculty group. While peer evaluations undoubtedly have professional improvement value, and while colleagues have an important stake in the maintenance of a respected faculty corps of quality, these seldom provide the substance needed for tough decisions and negative actions. Routinely administered student evaluations, which are behaviorally oriented, also offer as their principal value clues for individual self-improvement. The use of outcomes measures, touted in some circles, has many pitfalls. (These are discussed in another chapter.) Thus, an authority-based system may well be the only viable alternative in the light of certain legal considerations which are to follow.

TENURE AND DISMISSAL

Significance of Policies

Attainment of tenure should be one of the high points in any instructor's career. This is especially true in community colleges, which seldom offer opportunities to move up in faculty rank as do kindred universities. As significant as it is, tenured status should not be achieved through longevity alone. Tenure should come as a special action, appropriately recorded and with written notice and fanfare, following an evaluative and deliberative process. Personnel policies should so state, properly describe the process, and distinguish the rights and privileges of tenure as an official status.

For proper legal protection of the institution, policies should distinguish non-action, or failure to initiate a tenure granting action, as different from denial of tenure. In other words, tenure is not an *entitlement*, but rather a positive action exercised at the option of the institution. These same policies should also define clearly the meaning of probationary or temporary status, or any other terms employed by the institution. It should be clear that initial employment, and employment of non-tenured personnel, are for the extent of the contract period only, and that there is no obligation of either the college or the individual to extend or renew the contract or to offer another one.

As it will be noted in the section to come, certain legal assumptions tend to be made in the absence of clear policy statements. For these and other reasons, a well defined personnel policy structure in this area is extremely important in guiding institutional actions and protecting administrators and governing boards, as well as protecting the rights of individual employees.

Dismissal

According to Kaplin (1985), dismissal of staff tends to be governed under several different types of law. Among these are: contract law, labor relations law, constitutional law, and state statutes and regulations pertaining to public employment. One might hasten to add another body of "law": governing board policies properly drawn in accordance with legal constraints and within the laws granting powers to the board. Again, a disclaimer must be offered regarding the legal interpretations which follow, and the suggestion repeated that the use of legal counsel is necessary and appropriate.

Policies should say that a stated cause in not necessary in the nonrenewal of a contract of a temporary or probationary status employee. This non-action will not be subject to due process since no "property" interest is involved in failure to exercise an option to issue a new contract, and no "liberty" interest is at stake since no reasons are made public which adversely affect the faculty member's pursuit of life or career. (Board of Regents vs. Roth, 408 U.S. 564, 1972; and Perry vs. Sindermann, 408 U.S. 593, 1972) While it is clear that abstaining from any statement of cause which could be construed as "public" is wise under case law, as is avoiding private explanations of cause as well, since private conversations have a way of becoming public. This may seem harsh, but it is the safest practice.

The significance of policy becomes resoundingly clear in the case of *Perry* referred to above. This case involved the dismissal of a faculty member with lengthy service. The college in question declared officially that it had no tenure system, but in other declarations and communications *implied* that continuing employment was customary for those who performed their jobs creditably. The courts held that a system of *de facto* tenure existed, and that this "property" interest required due process. The same finding was evident in *Ferguson*, which speaks to "expectation" of continuing employment. (Ferguson vs. Thomas, 430 F2d 852, 5th Cir., 1970) In *Roth*, the courts held that in failure to renew a contract during the probationary period without a stated cause or a hearing at an institution with clear policies, none was required because no "liberty" or "property" interests were involved.

It is clearly to the institution's advantage to retain its legal options, although no one would condone arbitrariness in the exercise of these. These options are necessary if the college is to build and maintain strength in its instructional staff. It is inevitable that lack of information, misinformation, and even bad judgments will result in the selection of some staff who fail to meet performance standards.

On the other side of the coin, tenure has been much maligned as protecting the incompetent or as being simply outmoded in today's world. However, neither faculty nor administrators are quite ready to give up the protection of tenure. Tenure safeguards professional staff in the performance of their duties from arbitrary or whimsical treatment of superiors, whether in the administrative column or in governance. Further, there is still a need to protect the traditional rights of faculty in the pursuit and teaching of truth without intimidation or fear of unreasonable or irrational reprisal.

In public institutions, once tenure is granted or attained through policy default, it is protected under constitutional law. This constitutional protection includes the right of due process. Essentially, due process includes: (1) notice and a statement of applicable cause; (2) information as to the basis of infraction or cause; and (3) a hearing before an appropriate body, in which the affected person has the right to dispute evidence and offer defense. (Alexander and Solomon, 1972; Kaplin, 1985) It should be mentioned that dismissal of any employee within the term of a valid contract requires due process as well. While reference to college policies as stated in the handbook or in the policies and procedures manual be made in the contract or employment letter, inclusion therein is not obligatory providing such policies exist and are made available to staff. (Skehan vs. Board of Trustees of Bloomsburg State College, 501 F.2d 31, 3rd Cir., 1976)

Proper Cause

What constitutes proper cause? According to Alexander and Solomon (1972), the most commonly used cause is incompetency, yet this is one of the more difficult to define. Others include immorality, insubordination, and neglect of duty. Each of these causes may be much clearer to a court of law than they appear to a college administrator because each has a history in law and a relevant body of case law. Perhaps because of this, these and similar terms have tended to persist in statutory language where public employment protection exists at the state level, and college policies utilize such terms when prepared with the advice of legal counsel or modeled after those so prepared.

Nevertheless, within the limitations of any applicable statutes, college policies should define causes for dismissal. Wherever feasible and whenever advised by counsel, these more general causes should be defined in behavioral terms. Kaplin (1985) advises as follows:

> *Since incompetency, insubordination, immorality, unethical conduct, and medical disability are the most commonly asserted grounds for cause dismissals, institutions may wish to include in their dismissal policies definitions of these concepts and criteria for applying them to particular cases. Such definitions of these concepts or criteria should be sufficiently clear to guide the decision makers who will apply them and to forewarn the faculty members who will be subject to them.*

In preparation of policy statements the task is to make the causes for dismissal sufficiently clear as to avoid legal challenge on constitutional grounds of *vagueness*, but not so specific as to limit applicability to unique and different circumstances which arise and demand action. The following are examples, not necessarily models, of such definitions of cause:

1. *Permanent, chronic, or protracted physical or mental illness; or an impairment or condition which detracts from one's ability to perform his/ her duties; or a condition which substantially inconveniences college operations and functions, whether resulting from disease, accident, or other cause.*

2. *Personal misconduct; or unethical or unprofessional conduct; or failure to exercise professional courtesies and restraints; or conduct which materially affects one's value or usefulness to the college; or abuse of academic freedom as defined in college policies.*

3. *Professional incompetence or unfitness; or failure to perform one's duties in an acceptable manner; or capricious or unjust dealings with students; or failure to perform assigned duties or functions; or failure to fulfill time obligations or other commitments.*

4. *Such infraction of, or failure to obey, the law as materially and adversely to affect one's value or usefulness to the college.*

5. *Insubordination or non-cooperation affecting professional effectiveness or working relationships within the institution; or failure to observe defined or established institutional channels; or failure to follow institutional policies and procedures; or unwillingness to accept supervision; or failure to follow administrative directives, written or oral, when such administrators are acting within the purview of their authority or discretion.*

6. *Inability or unwillingness to adjust to changes in the college program, philosophy, or purposes.*

7. *Bona fide lack of need for one's full-time services; reductions or changes in courses or curriculum; changes in student enrollment patterns.*

8. *Bona fide necessity for financial retrenchment, as defined in staff retrenchment policies.*

9. *Failure to meet the standards and requirements for professional improvement as defined in college policies; failure to respond satisfactorily to evaluational shortcomings.*

While there is a considerable body of case law extending the meanings of the traditional legal terms for cause, there are other bodies of case law which establish limits. For example, there is case law which protects certain speech from constituting insubordination, but at the same time defining limits of that first amendment right. Case law also defines the limits of academic freedom. These appear complex, but as case law develops it tends to follow logic.

Some institutions have unnecessarily complicated their policies by including through reference broad, sweeping statements such as American Association of University Professors white papers. In so doing, they have broadened their policies to include considerable unidentified baggage. That is, they are including all of the case law regarding both the letter and intent of these statements. This is a magnanimous gesture, but a risky way to conduct college business.

CONCLUSION

There is a familiar illustration used among administrators about keeping one's mind on the mission of draining the swamp while in the midst of alligators. The moral imbedded in this story is certainly applicable within the academic personnel administrative milieu. While considerable concentration must be given to the avoidance of alligators, the administrative leader must never lose sight of the mission.

The mission of academic personnel administration and governance is, of course, the procurement and retention of highly qualified and competent faculty and other professional personnel. Of necessity, this involves not only selection processes designed and conducted in a manner compatible with the goal, but also the continuous professional development and growth of staff once acquired. Sadly, this mission also includes necessary purging of those who are unwilling or unable to perform in a manner contributory to fulfillment of essential college purposes.

Faculty are the front line forces, interacting directly with students in the teaching and learning processes. All other college services are in a sense supportive of this academic thrust. It is essential that administrative and other services focus upon providing an institutional climate conducive to effective instruction. Such an environment provides for needed freedoms, but also for needed system, order, and quality control. This is the challenge to leadership.

Topics for Discussion or Further Study

1. Make arrangements to obtain a definition of responsibilities for the personnel director or personnel office of a college with which you may be familiar. Do a critique of this statement.

2. What effects do unionization and collective bargaining tend to have on personnel recruitment and selection procedures? Is it necessary that these effects be deleterious to selection of good academic staff? Explain.

3. What type of master's degree is best for junior college teaching? Take a position and defend it.

4. Why do some criticize the doctorate as a teaching degree in the junior college? Discuss this issue in some detail.

5. Investigate the procedures for participation in personnel selection in two colleges. Compare and critique these. What changes would you make in each.

6. Write a position description for an announcement of vacancy for the position you occupy, or hope to occupy.

7. What is wrong with these interview questions?
   A. Do you have children? What are their ages?
   B. Do you have any illnesses or disabilities?
   C. Do you have a church affiliation?
   D. Are you planning a family soon?

8. What is meant by the term "collegial" when applied to a college?

9. Locate a form used for student evaluations. Critique this.

10. How does tenure protect a faculty member?

11. Research the issue of free speech and insubordination. Describe circumstances in which speech is protected and not protected.

INSTITUTIONAL RESEARCH & PLANNING

9

THE INSTITUTIONAL RESEARCH PROGRAM

Institutional research, and the reports and other data generated from quality efforts in this area, form the basis for institutional planning and administrative decision-making. Further, information derived from institutional research is the core of most proposals for external funding and support, for accreditation documents, and for much of the reporting a college must provide to its regulatory and governance agencies at the state level.

These internal studies offer interesting information for feedback into the local community. They assist in evaluation of institutional programs and performance of key functions. Institutional research assists the faculty in understanding their students and in the adaptation of instruction to student needs and characteristics. It provides information about the community and its needs which, in turn, affects the development of the curricular program of the college. In fact, little of consequence occurs within the college that does not in some way draw from the research it does about itself and its working milieu.

Smaller institutions may find it difficult to fund an independently identified office of institutional research with full-time professional staff and secretarial assistance. In such cases, this service office may be appropriately combined with certain other functions such as testing and counseling, admissions, institutional development (external fundraising), alumni relations, or with a faculty teaching assignment. Of the alternatives mentioned, the combination with a three to six credit hour teaching assignment is probably preferable in that it is less likely that the institutional research function will in practice be given second priority to other demanding duties. The planning function lends itself naturally to attachment with the institutional research effort.

In the following sections, the more obvious facets of a quality institutional research function will be discussed. However, those aspects which are related to entry assessment and evaluation of outcomes are discussed in a separate context in another chapter. This chapter will primarily deal with the types of studies conducted in a comprehensive program of institutional research.

The College Environment

Although not necessarily the first or most essential segment of an institutional research program, an appropriate point of departure for logical presentation is with the college environment. It is important that the institutional research office have in its files information about its service community and the broader environs of the state itself. It is expected that a community college should reflect the characteristics of its environment. This is not to say that the college should mirror its environment, but information should reveal that the college has been developed, and has plans for future development, which take into account community needs and community goals.

In its most simple form, the integration of college and community may be seen in the design of the campus and its buildings, in its naming, and in its promotional materials. In less obvious ways, rapprochement may be enhanced by the college curriculum, teaching approaches, nuances of student services, and constituencies of the governing board. It should be noted, however, that the college should reflect not merely the characteristics of the community along with the ideals, goals, and motivation of its people. The college must always be a pathway to individual goals, even those external to the community itself.

Some community information, as a result of self-initiated study or extraction from other documents, with which the institutional research office should be concerned include the following:

1. The Economic Environment (industries, employers, payrolls, job classifications, supply and demand for personnel, training levels and needs, property valuations, economic trends, economic development activities, economic impact of college).

2. The Socio-Cultural Environment (education system facts, fine arts groups, cultural activities, political and philosophical orientations, sensitive issues, local history information).

3. Area Demographics (population statistics including age distributions; income distributions; ethnic and racial distributions; mar-

riage, divorce, and family patterns; educational levels; job distribution patterns; public school populations by class with projections for future college entry).

4. Community Goals and Perceptions (goals for the college, stratified samplings of individual goals and needs, college image studies, quality perception studies, new directions studies, promotional impact evaluations).

While there may be other aspects of the community which can be studied and which may be highly significant for specific purposes, information in these general areas will provide the essentials for institutional planning and for maintenance of community/college integration.

Student Clientele

The college must know its student body. As important as it may be to know and understand the community served, it is even more important to know and understand that segment which has chosen to enroll for an education at the institution. Knowing and understanding implies more than the usual collection of facts, however significant those facts may be. It implies an understanding of the inner characteristics of these aspiring learners as well as a compilation of their significant numbers and categorizations.

Information about the students, if serving no other purpose, assists college officials and faculty in avoiding errors which are expensive in human potential, and perhaps dollars as well. Ignoring such information leads to errors in curricular programming, student services programming, planning, facilities development, and even in fundamental areas such as time scheduling. Understanding the student clientele will integrate the college with its community, and will assist in meeting the manifest needs of people. It will lead toward more efficient methods of providing educational experiences which are relevant to student goals.

The types of information a college needs to know about its student clientele are as follows:

1. Student Demographics (age, sex, marital status, socioeconomic levels, family income levels, ethnic and racial background).

2. Student Characteristics (ability levels; cultural, intellectual and social interests; employment status; value orientations).

3. Student Goals (educational goals, vocational goals, short and long-term goals).

4. Student Perceptions (perceptions and evaluations of the college and its services; self-perceptions; reality in goal setting).

5. Retention Studies (flow patterns of retention—full and part-time; fulfillment of declared goals; transfer patterns and timing— general, by program, and by clientele categorizations such as income or place-binding characteristics; contrast studies of retained and non-retained; dropout studies).

Studies of the student body, such as those indicated above, assure that the institution has fundamental knowledge of its clientele. While an institution may be fortuitous enough to intuitively plan and develop a program which is remarkable in its benefits for students, a conscientious effort to obtain and utilize significant data provides a much more reliable basis upon which to develop services.

Enrollment and Completion Patterns

Most computer software packages employed by college registration offices offer a data base which provides significant information about student enrollment patterns and trends. Such information is essential to scheduling, budgeting, and other functions critical to the efficiency of college operations. This information is also essential to evaluation and planning.

Some of the information needed in this area includes:

1. Enrollment Breakouts (day/evening; full-time/part-time; clientele characteristics as mentioned above; by entry period; by program, department, discipline; by declared student goals).

2. Enrollment Trends (day/evening; full-time/part-time, etc. as noted just above; graphing of various enrollment trends as well as tabulations).

3. Completions (completions of degrees and certificates; completion of declared goals; ratios of completion; completions broken out by various student clientele categorizations, including athletes - male/female).

4. Transfers (timing of transfers; transfers vs. completions; transfer institutions; transfer patterns and timing according to program; transfer patterns and timing by student clientele characteristics; success at transfer institutions).

5. Grades (grade point averages; grade point averages by program, department, and instructor; grade point averages by student clientele characteristics; trends in grade point averages; grade point by entry ability measures).

Any college which systematically produces studies of the nature described above is accumulating an impressively well documented record of its academic functioning. This record is subject to critical analysis and evaluation by the college administration, or by appropriate external groups such as accreditors. Further, such a record is filled with clues which may be gleaned in adjusting programs and planning for the future.

Administrative and Operational Studies

Various facets of administrative and other operations deserve some study and attention. Normally, such studies may be carried out by those in the offices of purview, but the institutional research office may be called upon for assistance in design, conduct, or reporting of such studies. Among those which merit some attention are the following:

1. Cost Studies (instructional costs by program; costs by student credit hour by discipline, department, program; costs per FTE on various breakouts; costs by unit of service in certain student services; cost trends by function within the college; cost trends by object internally; costs by instructional center; trends in total college costs per FTE student).

2. Facilities (utilization of classrooms, laboratories, special facilities; history and costs of facilities; institutional space according to type classification, age, condition).

3. Library Utilization and Holdings (by students; by faculty; by check-out and table; by students according to classification categories; books, academic periodicals, current popular periodicals, other media; holdings according to classifications and acquisition dates; courses which include library research assignments).

4. Faculty (qualifications and credentials; experience; graduate university of last credential; preparation in assignments; faculty loads by credit hours, contact hours; faculty loads by program, department; faculty loads by preparations; studies of released time; professional improvement activities of faculty; dates of last graduate study; advisement loads; participation in student orga-

nizations and activities; academic and professional activities, publications, organizational participation; academic organization and
community leadership roles; internal participatory records).

Studies of the type indicated above assure that there is adequate
information about the academic and business operations of the institution readily available for evaluation and use in self-examination and
adjustments necessary to an improving college. These studies also
provide a catalog of information frequently used in presenting in
planning, accreditation, or reporting documents.

Organization and Reporting

Too often, institutional research information is produced in raw
form as with computer printouts or compilations of rough statistics,
and filed in a dark place in an administrative office destined never to
see the light of a desk or to fulfill the enlightenment potential therein.
While some printout material is immediately useful in its generated
form, such is rarely useful to a busy president or other administrator
who must ferret out the meaningful from the rest.

For these and other reasons pertaining to a quality institutional
research effort, institutional research studies should be developed into a
series of reports or briefs. These might utilize a numbering and indexing
system based upon some adaptation of the classifications of research
presented in this chapter. This system should provide a basis for filing
in the research office as well as within other administrative offices.

An average institutional research report should be between two
and ten pages in length. Longer ones are likely to contain information
superfluous to the purposes of the administrator utilizing them. These
reports should present the nature of the study and its purposes,
present the factual findings in tabular and/or graphic form, include a
section on interpretations, and end with a discussion of implications.
The research office will, of course, accumulate resource documents
which are much longer, and may combine, compile, or integrate research reports into more comprehensive documents.

The gist of the above is that too much institutional research information will most likely go unseen, principally because it has not been
put into a conveniently usable format. The office responsible for institutional research should not expect other professionals within the
institution to be as delighted as they are by the fascinating tidbits
which these studies reveal. However, if it is appropriately presented
and packaged for use by others, the data are sure to receive considerable attention.

THE PLANNING FUNCTION

It is appropriate that some discussion of the planning function should follow the presentation on the institutional research program. The internal research product furnishes data which is essential to planning efforts. Planning which is attempted without appropriate information could be considered as merely organized and documented brainstorming. While the creativity associated with systemic brainstorming is certainly advantageous to planning processes, such must be done with factual reference points.

Practitioners sometimes tend to be dubious about the values of planning while theorists wax eloquent in praise. The argument most often heard among administrators in coffee sessions is that the planning process requires considerable time and resources and results in expensive documents which are out of date before the ink is dry. They point to the constantly changing environment within which colleges function and note that much of this change is not only beyond institutional control but unpredictable in its character and effects. Proponents argue that, without planning, institutions tend to drift and are apt to develop a reactive stance rather than a proactive one.

There is considerable merit in these arguments both pro and con, as to the planning function. Most administrators are well aware that planning has some values, and they understand that it is an integral part of a leadership position. Most who have been through a planning process, whether self-initiated or accomplished as a result of external influences, will admit that the effort was worthwhile.

There are several major inhibitors of institutional planning. It appears there is a lack of understanding regarding the process and what is actually involved. Some tend to see planning from the standpoint of an elaborate schematic, which would constitute investing an inordinate amount of time, energy, resources, and organization, and result in beautifully bound, elaborately illustrated documents. Some see it as a process which can only be carried out by a consulting firm costing vast sums of dollars. Some fail to differentiate between long-range planning and that which, at most, would be termed intermediate in length.

Perhaps these notions have been encouraged and amplified by attendance at seminars conducted by consultants who sell these type services. Encouragement may come from viewing the documents produced in larger, more sophisticated colleges with specialized personnel. Sometimes accreditors and other evaluators encourage an unrealistic perception of what constitutes appropriate and necessary planning.

The discussion which follows will touch on the essentials of planning. More detail may be found in a number of good resources on the subject. However, the practitioner will have to look upon these with caution since some will present planning as a very sophisticated process.

The Decennial Cycle

Once each decade, it is appropriate to engage in a planning process that is somewhat broader in its scope and coverage and which involves most of the basic constituencies of the college. This cycle may precede the ten-year regional accreditation review of the college, beginning two or three years in advance of the visitation. Or, some prefer to carry out this more involved type of planning at the beginning of each new decade of the calendar. The latter always provides a catchy title for the effort and for the resulting document.

The decennial planning effort is, of course, long-range in nature. Further, this form of planning is more visionary and less practical. The process involves a study agenda which focuses and directs the dynamics of organized groups from constituencies including administrators, faculty, support staff, governance, and the public of the community. This agenda focuses on where the institution should be and what it should become during the decade ahead. It requires mental freewheeling, unconstrained by immediate realities. Such efforts involve group dynamics, but may also include questionnaire studies broader than group participation.

The report document may reflect content such as that to be presented in the following section, including statistical summaries as indicated, but it will tend more toward a document of goals than a presentation of systematic plans for accomplishment of these. It will cover some of the same basic categories of institutional life, but may concentrate more on enrollment totals, curricular growth, expansions of student services, and facilities development. The decennial plan is highly speculative in nature. It is more visionary and might be characterized as "new horizons" in its orientation.

While requiring considerable time and relying upon good organization, decennial planning is certainly not beyond the expertise of most institutions. The key to a successful plan is in organizing the study groups, providing challenging but structured, focused agendas for their meetings, accurate recording of consensus of groups, and skill in compilation and writing.

Intermediate-Range Planning

Planning for an intermediate period normally targets a time of three to five years ahead of the present time. In practice, most of these are five-year plans with an update after two or three years. These plans are more action-oriented and realistic than decennial, or long-range plans. They involve a somewhat less elaborate organizational scheme, but do attempt to involve some representation of various college constituencies. This involvement may be in meetings or through responses to carefully prepared surveys. Again, input is sought, but will be sifted and refined by a smaller steering body to represent a plan which is optimistic but highly accomplishable.

The process may be similar to that described above, but the parameters are more limited and participation is less broad in scale. The resulting document is much more practical in its orientation.

The three to five year plan begins with an appropriate summarization of statistics as to where the institution is currently in the various facets of its operations, including enrollments, finances, facilities, programs, faculty, student services, and similar areas. The report then presents trends in each of these areas, followed by extrapolations. All this data, except the extrapolations, should come from institutional research studies performed regularly by that office. These should be prepared and presented in an appropriate format and made available for use in the planning process by discussion groups and as a basis for formulating any survey or study instruments prepared.

Essential to this planning process is a set of assumptions. Planning for the future is always based on some set of assumptions, whether in education, government, business, or personal life. Often these are null assumptions, i.e. assumptions that significant external and internal influences on the college will go unchanged. Sometimes planning is done on the basis that some elements of the influencing milieu will change and in definite ways. For instance, if it is expected that entrance requirements and tuition at nearby universities will be raised, then this assumption should be stated because it will influence both the enrollment and the characteristics of the college's students over the next few years. These planning assumptions are stated as an identifiable section within the resulting document.

While the components described above are in a sense a prelude, they are essential to any logically developed planning document.

The substance of the document is the presentation of planning goals and expectations. These are usually organized around the facets of college operations, but drawn from the data, trends, and extrapolations. A logical starting point is with enrollments, in general and by program. From these, further extrapolations and interpretations may be made as to the revision of the curriculum, needs for general and specialized space, needs for instructional staff, and needs for additional financial support as well as revised distribution.

Some documents integrate these needs and changes with the discussion and presentations of each operational component. However, it is well to present these in summary form in a stand-alone section. This section should also present any new thrusts anticipated and derived from the planning process. Further, this final section should present strategies and timetables necessary for accomplishment.

Because reproduction of the entire planning document may be expensive, many colleges design these final sections so that they may be reproduced alone and yet be meaningful to readers who may not have the entire document. This section is often distributed throughout the college's constituencies and governance.

Plans are, of course, made as charts for institutional development. These are a way of anticipating future changes and preparing to meet these challenges as they come. They provide for thoughtful, directed, strategic actions rather than the drifting and tangential courses taken by institutions which are simply buffeted along by unanticipated winds of change.

Topics for Discussion and Further Study

1. What should be the role of the president and/or other administrative officers in the program of institutional research? In the college planning program?

2. What sources can you identify that present clear information about the elements which make up a comprehensive program of institutional research?

3. From personal experience, or the experiences of professional acquaintances, and from the literature, cite the major arguments which may be made for and against extensive institutional planning efforts.

4. What differences might be expected in the characteristics of the planning process and the resulting documents in a small college as versus a large institution?

5. With what administrative offices might the director of institutional research have the closest working arrangements? Why? What offices might this director rely on most for support and encouragement?

PART THREE

The President's
Service Environment

ASSESSMENT & EVALUATION OF OUTCOMES IN ACCREDITATION

10

S ome might question the inclusion of a chapter on this in a book about the presidency. However, the attainment and the maintenance of accreditation is crucial to the welfare of the institution. Every president who expects recognition from within as the principal academic leader needs to be familiar with the accreditation processes for his college. While the president may delegate the organization and development of a comprehensive institutional research program, preparatory for the self-study and presentation of the college for accreditation, the leadership and guidance of his office is frequently necessary to accomplishment in this area. The president cannot afford to be inattentive to accreditation.

Further, assessment and evaluation have become the watchwords, and perhaps the current "buzzwords," within the higher education establishment. Effective leadership at the two-year college level must ultimately be judged not only according to the processes of productivity but also the product of the institution. While the input-output model lacks applicability in the educational development of human potential, useful parallels may be drawn from it. The material which follows involves an in-depth look at techniques which are applicable in student assessment and outcomes evaluation, especially as these pertain to accreditation by regional associations.

ANXIETY IS NORMAL

Coincident with several decades of experience in higher education and as a consultant-evaluator, this writer has frequently observed anxiety within the leadership of institutions when preparing for and undergoing the accreditation process. One might also add to the observation of general anxiety other traits best described as confusion, frustration, and misunderstanding. These conditions are greatly exacerbated each time there is an overhaul or announced change in the policies, procedures, and descriptive materials related to the accreditation process.

For those working most closely with accreditation, fear and confusion are not easily comprehended by those who are not. After all, are not the accreditation philosophy, rationale, procedure, and process presented clearly in the printed manuals and other materials? Has the new movement not been clearly enunciated and explained in the professional literature? Does no one read and study that which is available? Has the leadership within the accrediting body not explained the process and any proposed changes laboriously in meeting after meeting? The answer to all of these questions is normally in the affirmative. So, what is the problem?

The problem is one that has, most likely, existed forever in education. It is that of transfer of theory into practice. It is the understanding of theory as going beyond intellectualization and into application.

Quite often those who theorize and those who practice are divergent in their perspectives, and they are not really communicating with one another substantively. Sometimes those who theorize appear to eschew lowering themselves below the intellectual to the application level, as if some tarnish were involved. And, sometimes those who practice appear to resist policy by principle, rather than by rule, perhaps because rules have greater clarity, and tend to give comfort and security in compliance, while freedom tends to generate the anxiety associated with behavioral decisions.

WHAT'S NEW?

For more than a quarter-century most regional accrediting bodies have carefully avoided prescription. This is highly commendable. The accreditation rationale is presented in principle. Although published manuals are filled with suggestions clearly intended as explanatory of application, there has always been some anxiety associated with preparation for an accrediting examination. The new emphasis on assessment and outcomes measurement has given rise to heightened anxieties. It is appropriate to raise the question: "Is all this really new?"

There are those who may remember the earlier years when colleges were furnished long inventories designed to present the factual information about the institution desiring accreditation. Some may also recall that questions pertaining to assessment instruments and their use for guidance and placement of students were included, as well as questions about product evaluation and instruments employed. Did not the seven basic questions in vogue for the North Central region in 1965 ask about the accomplishment of college goals? And, current rationales have consistently pointed toward evidence of institutional mission accomplishment.

Institutional personnel have always been somewhat perplexed as to how to demonstrate college effectiveness in terms of outcomes. Consultant-evaluators, perhaps not too confident in these areas themselves and thus understanding the problems of college personnel, have accepted inadequate institutional research work in this area. However, pressed by internal and external forces, the regional accrediting groups are now saying that this component will receive more pointed attention and that institutions must meet the expectations outlined in the accrediting criteria.

In reality, the accreditation criteria demand little that institutional professionals should not be demanding of themselves. The self-study process, including the assessments suggested, requires only that the college give attention and effort to evaluation which most professionals recognize as needed, but which is preempted by everyday problems and crises. What quality institution's leadership does not desire to gather and employ appropriate information for placement of its students? What quality institution's leadership would not like to have in place a system for evaluating instructional outcomes more objectively?

ENTRY ASSESSMENT

For some years, vast numbers of institutions have required an entrance examination, such as that of the American College Testing Program, even though no cutting scores have been employed and no institutional admission decisions have necessarily been based on test performance. The new breakout of scores, called the Enhanced ACT, furnishes much needed information which should prove highly useful in the placement of entering students. Key areas for placement are in the two basic subjects: English and mathematics. This test, and other similar ones such as the ASSET (also by ACT) and ACCUPLACER (by Educational Testing Service), provide information of great value in these significant placement areas.

Colleges often go beyond such basic entrance batteries in meeting perceived student needs for proper placement within their curriculum. The ACT English and mathematics scores may be used to screen a large entry class into smaller groups according to abilities in these fields. These smaller groups would then given a home-based test specifically designed for placement in the college's unique course structure. This latter step is usually unnecessary, however.

Other instruments, such as a reading diagnostic tool, if not a component of the battery, may be added for those with lower scores on the pertinent entry tests in areas where reading and interpretation of materials are involved, and the results used for placement into a reading or study skills program. ACT also publishes the Study Skills Inventory, which may be useful for this purpose. Several of these instruments have automated computer scoring which can be done at the campus level for instantaneous availability of information.

In a few colleges, a general guidance battery is given to entering students either during the admission process or during the first semester. Such batteries frequently include a personality or adjustment inventory, a career interest instrument, and perhaps several specific aptitude instruments in areas such as verbal reasoning, numerical reasoning, spatial relationships, and the like. It should be noted that excessive testing of all students, beyond that which may have some value and relevance, is not recommended.

Some colleges also utilize computer guidance or testing programs which assist the student and/or the institution in clarifying goals and needs as a part of the guidance and counseling effort. A few may require completion of such a computerized program for all students. Some of these computer programs are quite sophisticated and well-regarded among guidance professionals.

It is obvious that even that segment of higher education which prides itself as "opportunity" oriented and as being "open door" in character, must engage in assessment processes for entering students if students are to be properly and efficiently served. Special assessment procedures may be relevant for the various technical and career programs which are encountered in the two-year college, and these specific programs may not always be "open door" in character. Nursing is a common example, but other complex technologies may each present entrance and placement problems which are unique. Generally speaking, and in the absence of other more obvious problems, programs with relatively low retention rates must be critically examined for entry assessment needs.

Newer instruments are emerging annually and institutional leadership should study the applicability of these as they appear. Some of these may offer possibilities of comparable pre and post tests, which will be discussed later in this chapter.

Again, institutions must avoid excessive or haphazard testing. Testing and other assessment efforts should have an educational purpose, directly related to the college's efforts at self-improvement or to serving the students' needs. Accrediting groups and evaluators will not expect assessment procedures which go beyond good professional practice. Assessment programs should have a rationale which can readily be explained to both internal and external groups.

FOLLOW-UP STUDIES

One of the most common forms of scholastic product evaluation is the follow-up study of graduates and school leavers.

Most career education programs with good leadership conduct these follow-up studies regularly. These consist of a set of questions mailed to graduates or recipients of specified credentials after these have been out in the world of work for six months to one year. A few do repetitive studies after two and five years. These should be geared not only to evaluate the student's transition and success but also to analyze the curriculum and courses of study for strengths and weaknesses.

Proper evaluation procedure for career students includes contact with the employers. Traditionally this has been by questionnaire, but reports in the field indicate that employers are becoming increasingly reluctant to provide written evaluations as the legal aspect of doing so has become more threatening. It is suggested that very short and succinct questionnaires which focus strictly upon the training aspects may have greater success, or better yet, that this data be obtained by standard telephone interview rather than by questionnaire.

Follow-up studies of transfer students is also appropriate, particularly of those who receive an associate degree designed for transfer (arts or sciences). Of course, transfer students studies depend heavily upon the cooperation of the receiving institutions. Generally speaking, data which will allow the sending college to compare the grade point averages of transfer students at both institutions is desirable. However, both institutional authorities and accrediting evaluators must be aware of the phenomenon called "transfer shock," and thus the tendency for junior college transfer students to have an initial drop. Information which will allow the sending institution to compare the upper-division success of transfer students with native students according to grade point earned during the first two years is the best for making evaluative judgments, but this is often difficult to obtain.

One type of follow-up study, not often done but necessary in two-year colleges, is the follow-up of students who are placed in reading, study skills, and other developmental courses. Most junior colleges are committed to a philosophy of serving all comers through placement in developmental offerings which are designed to give these students with limited academic backgrounds an opportunity to overcome deficiencies and move into the academic mainstream if they have the potential and the motivation. Usually there is an untested assumption that these are effective. It is a good idea to test this assumption with follow-up research. However, it should be noted that both college leaders and evaluators must be prepared to accept low success rates without passing quick judgment that the opportunity for these students should be withdrawn.

The results of these follow-up studies should be properly reported. Too often follow-up information is kept in loose- leaf form in a folder, perhaps with some hand tabulation, until someone asks for it. An institutional research summary report should be prepared and distributed internally to those who need to know its contents. These summary reports should present basic information, perhaps in tabular format, along with an interpretation and analysis. A condensation of results should be reported in the college's self-study document, and a rack containing copies of the series of institutional research reports should be available in a room set aside for the visiting team during an evaluation. This same suggestion is applicable to all institutional research studies.

RETENTION STUDIES

Retention studies are difficult to design, and often difficult to interpret as a result of the way they are designed. The institution must first contemplate what it wants to learn and/or to demonstrate from such data.

These purposes may vary according to the agency or authority requesting the information. Sometimes institutional administrators and other personnel find themselves in what is sometimes called a "Catch 22" situation. Many of the nation's colleges are under an indictment of sorts for the failure rates or low graduation rates of their students, particularly of minority groups. Nevertheless, other pressures from financial aid regulators, tax-payers' groups, and standards movements bear heavily upon institutions to raise academic requirements, raise grading standards, and eliminate the non-performers more quickly.

Essentially, the institution needs to know what happens to every student who enrolls. For instance, for the fall semester each member of the entering freshman class either: (1) drops out during the semester; (2) completes the semester and: (a) drops out; (b) transfers; or (c) re-enrolls. This process continues on for four to eight (or more) semesters in the junior college.

Most colleges try, at least sporadically, to study the causes of dropouts. The results of these usually show a high percentage of dropouts for financial reasons (a socially acceptable, as well as an honest answer to queries), personal reasons (family, marriage, etc.), health factors, and so on. Some will admit academic problems. What is usually not asked, and should be asked, is whether or not the individual completed his/her own objective for enrolling.

Dropout data for junior colleges may be misinterpreted because so many students enroll only part-time, and so many have very limited objectives for attending. This information obviously has different meanings for full-time, versus part-time students, and retention statistics as well as dropout studies should be made separately. Further breakouts may also be interesting and useful, such as by program or by demographic categorizations.

One significant question which retention studies should answer for institutional evaluation purposes relates to the academic differences between those who are retained and those who are not (discounting transfers and goal-completers). The college should be able to show evidence that the academically able are being retained. This is best done through statistical comparison of the entry test scores of each group and the grade point averages of each group. Essentially, it is this academic evidence, along with information regarding former students, that is of most interest to evaluators.

PRODUCT (OUTCOMES) EVALUATION

Colleges of all levels have long sought a means of conducting an objective evaluation of the achievement of general education goals and objectives. Unfortunately, standardized tests did not exist in the past which were tailored for this at the institutional goal level. And, unfortunately, standardized tests do not exist currently which are tailored toward each institution's general education objectives. Nevertheless, better and more appropriate test batteries have been emerging, and more will likely be forthcoming. Most of these have merit for consideration in the evaluation of educational outcomes, and this alternative should not be rejected simply because available tests have limitations.

The writer once instituted a standardized testing study of general education outcomes in a university setting utilizing the General Culture Tests, although these were not designed to measure that institution's goals and objectives. However, the results of the testing program showed the university's students fell short of the norms in the arts and humanities areas while being relatively ahead in the sciences. Certainly, this provided information of considerable significance to curriculum planners within that institution.

Similarly, an outcomes evaluation process for sophomores in transfer-oriented programs, utilizing a nationally standardized instrument with broad general education coverage and a normative group generally representative of the nation's two-year college sophomores, will reveal information of great significance to both institutional personnel and accrediting evaluators. The Academic Profile, a new sophomore level battery by Educational Testing Service, yields breakout scores in the common areas of general education, such as humanities, social sciences, natural sciences, mathematics, and writing. It also has scores for reading and critical thinking. The existence of such an effort, and evidence of use of data obtained in curricular and academic adjustments, should be positives for any college undergoing accrediting evaluation, regardless of score levels.

It is well, however, to sound a mild caution that such results require careful and restrained interpretation. Each institution must remain free to set its own general education objectives, as long as these are in the broad bounds of academic theory and practice, and to design a curriculum to bring these to fruition. Each institution will not be equally strong in all areas, nor will graduates of different programs within an institution be consistently profiled. These tests are likely to be inappropriate for Applied Sciences (career) students. Certainly, sophomores of two-year colleges with non-selective enrollments must not be negatively compared with sophomores of institutions with selective processes at entry. Even the existence of a nearby upper division institution tends to cause the more able students to become early transfers thereby affecting the quality of the graduating sophomore group. There are very subtle socioeconomic influences at work in some situations. The results for any college must be viewed with consideration for its entry clientele, as well as its mission and curricular emphases and other less observable influences.

Perhaps a further word of caution is in order regarding pressures nationally and movements within some states toward standardized testing programs which may include a general education battery for sophomores or a "rising junior" examination. If comparative judgments are made, and if these tests or the tendency to compare, in turn lead to the loss of autonomy in general education program planning and course content determination, basic philosophical principles are at stake. Two-year colleges must resist such efforts leading to downward prescription and concomitant loss of academic freedom. Further, caution should be exercised lest the tests dictate the curriculum. This is apt to occur when external stress is placed upon the results obtained.

The "value added" concept has received some attention among collegiate theorists and has been tried in some institutions. This approach holds much promise in theory, but presents problems both in application and interpretation. To measure "value added" as a result of collegiate learning experiences students are given the same test (or carefully constructed and equivalent alternate forms) at entry and exit. The difference is the value added, presumably as a result of instruction. These tests usually cover various areas of general education, but the approach might be applied to any program where instruments exist, including specific disciplinary areas.

Complications arise as decisions are made as to the basis for comparison. If the tests are the same (or equated in terms of item point selection, item by item difficulty level, and item by item discrimination indices) then raw scores may be subtracted. If test form equivalency is statistically determined, as is normally the case, then standard scores (not raw scores and not percentiles) may be subtracted. Once the subtractions are made, then interpretation becomes the problem. If these score differences (raw or standard) are to be interpreted relative to either entry or sophomore norms, then the larger percentile differences result from comparisons made to distances in and around the median. (Percentiles are unequal units.) As an added complication, some institutions may take the average scores made by all entering students and compare these with the average scores made by all (surviving) sophomore students. This, of course, adds in the selective retention factor and confuses the issue entirely. These complexities and associated confusion bring to mind the adage that "figures don't lie but liars figure." The process employed must be clear to institutional personnel and to evaluators, and it should be professionally acceptable.

Of course, the simplest way of evaluating the results of pre and post testing is to compare the relative (percentile) standing of the group of sophomores on sophomore norms with this identical student group on entry compared with entering student norms. If the test company has properly normed the test, this comparison is valid. But, again, a word of caution is appropriate. The institution is looking toward students maintaining essentially the same standing. An improvement is, of course, a plus, but slight changes in either direction (commonly found) are unlikely to be statistically significant. In order to claim a real difference, a statistical test would have to be performed (using standard scores). One must remember that the goal is to stay relatively even, or, if the surviving group has scored significantly below the middle upon entry, to show that they have progressed toward the middle. Anything more is a bonus.

In actual practice, most test batteries are geared either for the purpose of assessment and placement of entry students or for the purpose of evaluation of sophomores or higher classes in the attainment of certain skills. This means that these tests do not overlap to the extent that a direct comparison, such as that discussed above, is educationally and statistically appropriate. A variation, which may be employed in the absence of more appropriate pre and post test data, is the statistical (or normative) comparison of the results of two different test batteries administered before and after.

Thus, an institution with entry test data on hand from an achievement battery, the content of which is inappropriate for sophomores (ceiling effects, curricular content, etc.) or which has no appropriate sophomore form or norms, may administer a different test which covers similar broad areas of content to sophomores. By converting both sets of scores into the same standard score system (based upon the standard deviations), a statistical comparison of means of these standard scores may be made, in addition to the usual examination of class medians in relation to each separate chart of percentile norms. This tells the researcher and others whether these students have maintained their same relative position on both instruments. The presumptions are that both have been broadly and representatively normed, and that they represent measures generally within the same broad areas of achievement (although at different levels of content). As indicated, this is a substitute methodology when time is lacking for longitudinal study, or proper instruments are unavailable (as is often the case), and it utilizes data which may be on file. It has assumptions which may not be wholly reliable, but it can provide useful clues to academic progress under circumstances exhibiting the practical restraints cited.

Perhaps a word is in order about proficiency testing, or what may be known as basic (minimum) academic competency testing. Minimum competency testing most frequently occurs in the two basic tool areas of English (usage or writing) and mathematics. Sometimes this is for the purpose of guiding the poorly performing student into further study, but it may be for the purposes of assuring the basic competency of all degree recipients, transfers, or upper division students (rising juniors). The purpose/s of minimum competency testing are different than the measurement of learning outcomes, but there may be some relationship. Measures of minimum competency are theoretically designed to assure that a *basic* standard of achievement has been met, as versus a *desirable* level. Theoretically these tests would contain only basic, as versus advanced, content or material. Scoring tends to be on a pass/fail basis, with a tendency for the dividing line to be somewhere around a "D" performance level. Such tests would presumably have cutting scores based upon subjectively established criteria, as versus normative data, although in actual application normative data are often used to establish the criteria.

Certain tests, namely the Academic Profile (by ETS), have proficiency (criterion) scoring in areas such as writing, mathematics, and reading/critical thinking, as well as normative scores in the usual areas of general education. The CAAP (Collegiate Assessment of Academic Proficiency by ACT) breaks out proficiency in writing, mathematics, reading, critical thinking, and scientific reasoning, although it appears to have normative scoring.

Again, the institution and its personnel must establish the purposes to be accomplished by the testing program. Then the selection of instruments must follow these purposes.

The evaluation of programmatic learning outcomes, while at times appearing to defy assessment, may actually be more simple than the evaluation of general education outcomes. In four year colleges and universities, the use of the Graduate Record Examination (but not graduate program entry norms, which are obviously more selective than senior norms) may be appropriate, and teacher competency exams as well as other senior program tests are available. In two-year colleges licensure examinations sometimes provide critical data.

One comment should be made regarding the record of graduating students on licensure examinations, such as nursing. A perfect record is not necessarily desirable. Colleges boasting a 100% pass rate are quite obviously failing some students who would have passed if given an opportunity. Pass rates of 90% or so are indicative of a more humane approach to standards. Further, pass rates should be expected to vary from year to year.

But evaluation of career and technical education program outcomes is not limited to test results. Technical programs often involve projects or products of student work. A "jury" of persons drawn from the career field may be asked to judge student projects. Similarly, such a jury may be requested to come into the classroom or laboratory and administer certain "tests" or tasks associated with job performance and to judge students' performance on these. If properly handled, quantified, and reported, either or both of these procedures may offer strong evidence regarding the quality of learning outcomes. Such evidence may, of course, be more valid in some ways than test information, although it is more subjective and lends itself to manipulation and bias.

Program area tests for junior college students in their academic majors may be quite difficult to find. Take, for example, the business area. Most arts and sciences program tests are geared to testing senior students rather than sophomores. Until instruments are available for this purpose, institutional researchers may have to turn to other methods which are less direct and less objective. It should be mentioned that certain disciplinary associations or groups, such as chemistry and economics, have developed tests for use in assessing outcomes of basic two course sequences in the field. While these may have standardization weaknesses, they should prove useful in content areas where they are available.

OTHER EVALUATIVE STUDIES

Before leaving the topic of evaluation of technical and career education programs, it is appropriate to consider another form of study which yields evidence of suitability and quality in this area. This is the curriculum evaluation.

It is often suggested that, in order to keep the curriculum and the courses of study current in career programs, these programs should be periodically critiqued by an advisory committee consisting of persons employed in the field or supervising others who are employed in the field. These critiques are often informal and in the form of discussions, but they may have much greater acceptance as a method of evaluation if a more formal approach is taken.

Elements of an evaluation of a career curriculum by its advisory committee or some other appropriate jury panel include an evaluation of the program's stated objectives as to clarity, appropriateness, accomplishability, and relevance. Each course, specialty or general education, is evaluated on its contribution to program objectives and needed adjustments (if any). The program as a whole is evaluated as to how well it prepares students for job entry, its comprehensiveness, evidence of planning and design, implementation of objectives in the curriculum, and preparation of students for advancement beyond entry level positions. Most institutional researchers, with the assistance of program personnel, are quite capable of developing some similar format for career program curriculum evaluation.

These procedures will need endorsement and active participation by administrative leadership. Since evaluation is often threatening to program instructional personnel, these efforts will likely require a boost from those in charge.

A evaluative procedure often used, although the rationale is not always made clear, is the survey of institutional climate. While there are rather comprehensive versions of these available commercially with scoring services and profiles provided, most colleges develop their own versions. Either approach is appropriate. Essentially, these surveys attempt to obtain the opinions and the assessments of students and/or faculty to various aspects of the college milieu and services rendered by the college. Commercial versions are usually focused on the more subtle, pervasive, psycho-social characteristics of the institutional climate as felt by students or faculty, while institutional versions are usually shorter and more pointed toward a mental reaction to the various practical and obvious facets of college operations. Either may provide insights into internal dynamics.

The evaluation by graduating students may be the most practical version of the above. Well-constructed instruments are often devised by institutional personnel or obtained through the borrowing and trading process with other colleges which obtain needed demographic identity, program area, reasons for attending, factors in attraction, personal and academic status at entry, and go on to request evaluation of advisement, counseling, instructors/instruction generally and in the major field, general education, library, physical aspects of classrooms and labs, financial aids services, admissions process, administrative services, grading practices and activities program. While these student evaluations may have a bias in favor of the college, and may be criticized as unscientific quantification of the opinions of those unqualified to make judgments, they are nevertheless just what they are purported to be—the assessments made by graduating student consumers. And, as such, these have some validity.

Informally developed faculty and staff surveys are also employed in presenting information about the institution or in attempting to provide evidence of institutional quality. For the latter these have dubious merit, but for the former such inventories may be quite useful. It is significant, of course, to quantify faculty thinking and opinion, as well as to collect factual information. Faculty reactions to working conditions, such as loads, support services, office arrangements, and their views on percolation of ideas, academic freedom, internal governance, salaries and benefits, professional growth opportunities, and the like are of considerable significance. These studies, if properly organized and reported, are useful internally, as well as to accrediting evaluators. These are not outcomes measures, however. These studies offer information relevant to a criterion other than that which seeks evidence of accomplishment of mission, namely that which addresses the presence of conditions which will lead toward mission accomplishment.

Faculty grading studies are often a part of comprehensive institutional research programs, yet there exists some quandary about their value or usefulness in evaluating outcomes. Grade inflation tends to be a universal problem in all types of institutions. Student grade points averages around 2.7 (on a 4.0 scale) are the norm. If the college's average grade point is near that, does it mean that the faculty is in line with national trends? If the college's average grade point is higher, does this mean that better instruction and/or better learning is occurring? If the college grade point is lower, does this mean that the faculty makes stronger academic demands and has tougher standards, or that students are learning less? In the absence of other information, some of it corroborative, it is difficult to interpret grading studies. Generally, one must be somewhat suspect of higher student grade point averages when the entry group's test scores are considerably below average. Certainly, high grade point averages in the face of below average sophomore test results would be suspect.

Grade point studies do have value as an internal consistency check, and in identifying areas which merit further attention and study. An avid institutional researcher might find some interest in correlational studies of grade points by field with sophomore test results by corresponding area. Or, a sophisticated researcher might develop a correlation matrix of entry test scores, sophomore test scores, and grade points by field, and proceed to partial out the influence of the entry scores (hold them statistically constant), and observe the retained correlational relationship. This could be theoretically, and mathematically, similar to the "value added" concept.

Formally organized surveys of citizen opinion are usually both interesting and useful to evaluators, as well as to college authorities. These may have several different purposes and may address different segments of the institutional clientele. They may assume quite different formats.

One form of citizen survey seeks a validation of institutional mission and purposes. This is usually a straightforward presentation of college purposes, including perhaps some divergent or extraneous ones, asking for response as to the degree of agreement or disagreement on something similar to a Likert Scale. Usually the results of such studies support the declared purposes of the college, as might be expected. The levels of agreement often are clues to citizen priorities, and the rejection of extraneous purposes supports a view that citizens understand the college mission better than is sometimes believed.

Citizens may be asked to rate the quality of instructional services, administrative leadership, and programs by broad category (such as general education or career education). They may also be asked to rate the degree to which the college is accomplishing certain of its specific purposes. General reactions of citizens may be obtained as to their supportiveness of this option for student education, the clientele appropriately served, economic impact on the community, general contributions to quality of life, and so on. Sometimes an "image" study is included, which may use statements for agreement or disagreement or even utilize an adjective checklist format.

Citizen surveys are most frequently addressed to opinion leaders within the college service area. However, these may be designed with stratified or random sampling, or they may be directed toward certain subgroups such as minorities, employers, housewives, or other special groups the college seeks to serve.

Again, the value of these surveys lies not in the presence or lack of scientific method of inquiry and statistical analysis, but in the face validity which the results embody as quantifications of opinion. Favorable responses, whether these be in agreement with elements contained in the mission statement or choice of positive adjectives to describe the college's image, are indicative of local support for its efforts.

This paper does not purport to address all forms of institutional research which may be significant internally or significant in presenting the institution for accrediting evaluation. There are other studies which are of great value. An example is that of a comprehensive study of the student clientele served, as well as an analysis of potential clientele unserved or under served. Community demographics are important. The college mission is actualized through its curriculum and its program of services to the clientele it seeks to serve. The material and analysis presented in the self-study document for accreditation should indicate the integral relationship of mission, instructional and service program, clientele, and community. The accreditation rationales are usually quite simple. Generally, these ask that the college define its mission, show that the resources and conditions necessary to mission accomplishment are present, provide evidence indicating mission accomplishment, and demonstrate that the college will continue to accomplish its declared purposes.

A SAMPLE TESTING PROGRAM

Choices of instruments should be integral with institutional philosophy and purposes. Tests are merely instruments of purpose within an overall assessment program, which should be drawn from institutional thought. Nevertheless, a rudimentary testing effort within a junior college might include the following:

Entry level:

The Enhanced ACT. Yields English score broken out in mechanical usage and rhetorical for English placement. Yields mathematics score broken out for pre-algebra, elementary algebra, intermediate algebra, geometry, and trigonometry for mathematics placement. Yields reading score broken out to prose, humanities, social sciences, and natural sciences, for screening in reading skills. Also yields scientific reasoning score.

ACT Study Skills Inventory. To be given only to those with low scores on the reading test above.

Sophomore level:

The Academic Profile (ETS). Yields scores for the evaluation of general education outcomes in humanities, social sciences, natural sciences, mathematics, writing, reading, and critical thinking. Yields criterion scores in reading/critical thinking, writing, and mathematics.

CONCLUSION

The purpose of this chapter is to present a translation of assessment and evaluation principles pertinent to accreditation evaluation in practical terms for institutional leadership faced with the challenge of pending review. The intent is to describe in a pragmatic fashion some of the more promising procedures and techniques for meeting both the criteria of good professional practice and the expectations of accrediting evaluators. This chapter does not purport to be officially descriptive of policy of any specific accrediting body, nor does it attempt in any way to speak for these agencies. If it has some value as a practical, but not prescriptive, guide for developing at least a rudimentary program for student assessment and evaluation of outcomes, then it has accomplished its objective.

While the views and procedures described may appear elementary to some and technical to others, these ideas should be useful to those struggling with planning and developing institutional research programs with a view toward accreditation processes. This knowledge could prove invaluable to a president who has entered into office without past experience with institutional research and accreditation policies and practices.

Topics for Discussion or Further Study

1. Why should the president be concerned with the program of assessment and evaluation in the institution?

2. From the literature, write a two page paper outlining and describing the elements of a comprehensive institutional research program in the two-year college.

3. In what ways should institutional research be utilized in strategic planning and decision making within a college?

4. If your personal interest is in an occupational program, design a suitable program for assessment of outcomes in that field. If your interest is in an academic or general education area, design an outcomes evaluation program for that sector.

5. Why does the author caution about externally imposed evaluation programs?

6. Is the "value added" approach a simple one? Why? Why not?

7. Design a testing program which would aid in assessment and evaluation in an institution with which you are familiar.

8. What dangers are inherent in the use of cutting scores?

9. Design a student follow-up questionnaire for your area of interest.

10. In what ways might entry assessment procedures run counter to the "open door" community college philosophy? In what ways might this not be true?

THE NON-URBAN JUNIOR COLLEGE

11

Since a number of the principles embodied in this book are most applicable in the non-urban community college setting, it is appropriate to take an in-depth look at this particular segment of the nation's two-year colleges. In 1976 the directors of the American Association of Community and Junior Colleges, in response to formal and informal expressions of several hundred of its constituent institutions, formed the Task Force on Small/Rural Community and Junior Colleges. This was followed by the formation of the Commission on Small/Rural Community and Junior Colleges, a permanent subdivision of that organization. This writer was fortunate enough to have served on the task force and was the principal author of its published report.

The task force was to "focus on issues of concern to community colleges enrolling small numbers of students but serving large geographic areas." Position papers emerged dealing with topics such as equal opportunity, fiscal affairs, accreditation, and research needs. The final report synthesized most of these into a single document. Many of the ideas expressed here are traceable to this source, as published in the *Community College Review* under this author's name.

WHAT IS RURAL?

Academicians often feel uncomfortable without a proper definition of terms. The vagueness of the basic term of reference, "rural," is a source of such discomfort. What is rural? Are the problems associated with being rural essentially the same as those of being small, since most rural institutions (and a few urban ones) are indeed small? Is a college with an enrollment of 1,500 in a small city of 35,000 rural? Is rural a broad category into which all institutions other than those distinctly urban fit? Is the size of the total population base or its centrality of location the criterion of urban/rural differentiation? What about suburban institutions? Is the size of the enrollment or the size of the population served the basis for classification?

The task force was not able to resolve all of these questions. Instead the members moved toward an operational definition that a rural community college is one which is regarded as such by its own leadership. Basically, the task force thought of the rural community college as publicly supported, located in a center of under 100,000 population, and serving a broad geographic area with a program having an identifiable thrust toward comprehensiveness.

There is some variance in reported statistics and estimates of how many rural community colleges there are in the United States. This may be because of the different definitions being employed, the ambiguity of enrollment data in the reporting of part-time students, and the lack of nationwide surveys or studies of relevance to this sector. In general terms, it would be safe to state that there are probably more than 700 rural or non-urban community and junior colleges in the nation. More than 600 of these are public institutions. In excess of half of the membership of AACJC could be regarded as rural under the broad definition cited above. Approximately half of the rural institutions are located in population centers of 10,000 or under. Some two-thirds of these colleges enroll fewer than 1,000 students.

If these statistics have any level of credibility whatsoever, one must be impressed by them. The sheer number of such institutions is impressive, and their potential impact in service communities across the nation is overwhelming. Certainly this important and significant sector of public education deserves attention and examination by educators, researchers, and public policy making bodies at all governmental levels.

THE RURAL MILIEU

The often-held concept of urban superiority and rural inferiority is one which is becoming increasingly resented by rural people, including community college presidents. This view is deeply ingrained in the culture and has been reinforced by literature, films, music, and other forms of art and media. Like other prejudicial attitudes, it may manifest itself in ways which are subtle and difficult to recognize. The neglect experienced by this sector of higher education is likely more benign than deliberate in nature.

Interestingly, it has been cited that, with two exceptions, every American president in this century has been either born or reared in a small town, a trend of early history which has endured despite urbanization.

However, all is not well in rural America. It has been estimated that as many as one-third of rural Americans live within or on the borderline of poverty. The average age of rural Americans is increasing. Small town businesses and small towns are dying. More than ninety percent of those counties suffering from critical manpower shortages are rural. With one-fourth the population, rural areas have more than half the substandard family housing.

Some optimists point to a few indicators that suggest things will get better in the future for this sector. Concern for preservation of the ecology and a passion for the natural and the historical have led to a revival of interest in rural areas. Something of a reversal in population trends has been noticed. Rural development is given impetus by the current move toward diversification and relocation within the industrial sector. Some people are seeking a simpler life with less violence, pressure, and pollution and more space, green grass, and fresh air.

THE RURAL JUNIOR COLLEGE

Rural America, the conservatory of social traditions, has been neglected from the perspective of particular problems which confront sparsely populated areas where only limited opportunities for employment, cultural activities, and comprehensive social services exist. The community college represents a potential catalyst for addressing many of the problems of rural life whose solutions may lie in the education and development of people. Consistent with the purposes of the community college are the initiation and implementation of programs and services which could enhance educational, economic, cultural, recreational, and civic development in rural areas in the years ahead. Various mitigating circumstances interfere with role actualization.

Some of the problems found by small colleges in a rural setting include the impoverishment of cultural, social, and recreational services in the area; the lack of part-time jobs for students and positions for graduates; program comprehensiveness with a limited total enrollment; the various inefficiencies of physical smallness; attracting and developing staff; competition in procurement of grants and other funds; conforming with intricate federal and other regulatory requirements; financial stress; community financial crisis related to lack of diversification of the economic base; lack of time and expertise to research local problems; communications problems in a lightly populated area; housing of students; lack of exposure and visibility in the media at the various capitals and within higher education and the community college movement; lower educational levels of parents and other adults; and a weak economic base caused by property values scattered over a wide geographic terrain.

Rural community colleges frequently face problems of status and problems of competition within the higher education system and with their own larger and more prosperous peer institutions. Small rural institutions lack the clout with legislative bodies and regulatory agencies that universities, four-year colleges, and their big sister colleges in the cities appear to have. Some believe small, rural institutions receive less attention from the organizations to which they belong. Others believe that accrediting bodies are dominated by their larger metropolitan counterparts. Rules and formulae for division of funds for operations and for facilities fail to consider the smaller college's unique problems and circumstances. Government requirements of statistics, surveys, and report documents often seem silly, as well as unreasonably burdensome, to a small, overworked administrative staff. Researching the professional literature reveals few solutions to problems, for these are the unmentioned institutions. The higher educations journals are almost as silent as if this vast sector of higher education did not exist.

Leaders in rural community colleges are becoming increasingly activist in their style. They have become more outspoken in meetings. They are demanding that the establishment within the realm of education, and the power structure within government, become responsive to their concerns and the problems of their constituency. This book, and particularly this chapter, may be viewed as such an expression.

EQUAL OPPORTUNITY

One of the fundamental philosophical tenets upon which the American democracy is founded is that of equal opportunity. The political system, economic system, and social institutions all reflect this basic value. Throughout the two hundred years of the nation's history, the meaning of this premise of equal opportunity has been constantly expanded by both legal and extra-legal change. Since equality of educational opportunity underlies all other forms of individual liberty to attain one's goals in life, it is incumbent upon a democratic society to bring such opportunities within the reach of all, regardless of economic class, ethnicity, or any other element of circumstance—including geographic isolation.

The rural family is often penalized in respect to higher education, since geography has been found to be a major factor in determining who goes to college. Examinations of the enrollments of community colleges reveal a predominance of local students. It has been reported that enrollments decline proportionally as far as fifteen miles from a junior college campus and become almost nonexistent at fifty miles. It has also been shown that the percentage of high school graduates going on to college in the vicinity of a junior college is much higher than in areas where there is no such institution. Thus, geography, the junior college, and educational opportunity are all closely intertwined.

Public policy making bodies in each state must face squarely the issue of conflict between this fundamental human right, so well established in the legal system and in the beliefs of the people, and the limited resources which are available for implementing the principle in the educational delivery system. Many public bodies holding such responsibilities have failed to consider this issue of access or have done so only superficially.

This principle was stated by the Task Force as follows: "Equal educational opportunity demands that public policy-making bodies provide for comprehensiveness in curriculum and in services in all community college units regardless of size or geographic location." The provision of a reasonable diversification of curriculum has been considered almost as important as maintaining a geographic dispersal of institutions.

The community college represents a unique American effort to democratize higher education. This assumes, as did Thomas Jefferson, that education is necessary to the preservation of democracy, that education has a principal role in societal change, and the role of education in upward social mobility helps to equalize opportunities for all who come under its range of vision. Thus, the community college is an important instrument of a democratic government in assuring a basic right to its citizens.

FINANCE

Anyone who has ever been exposed to a course in economics, and even most who have never been inside a college classroom, recognize the economy of size in business, church, or other endeavors. Surely those in positions of leadership and policy making in higher education should understand such a concept exceedingly well. Nevertheless, funding formulae abound across the nation which ignore or deny this truth. Interestingly enough, many of these funding systems are justified by a rationale of treating each institution alike.

Perhaps it is something of a paradox to suggest that such ideas of fairness are grossly unfair. Nevertheless, any system of division of resources among institutions which is based upon equal funding per unit is an inequitable system and is prejudicial against the smaller community college. This is true whether the unit is that of FTE student, average daily attendance, student credit hours, student contact hours, credit hours by program, students by program, or most of the other commonly practices systems of this kind.

Some of the considerations are worthy of further note. In staffing, one specialist is required regardless of program size. Certain special programs require a laboratory and special equipment regardless of enrollment. The library must have holdings supportive of the curriculum irrespective of numbers. Space utilization ratios will be lower. Certain other costs tend to be fixed at a base level, such as administration, physical plant operation, and student activities.

The Task Force set forth the principle that equity in funding as a means of equalizing educational opportunities among the organizational units of any state system of public and community colleges depends upon the inclusion of some means, mathematical or other, of allowing for the higher costs of operation per unit within the smaller, rural community college.

ACCREDITATION

Perhaps leaders from smaller colleges spread some kind of contagion of group paranoia as they meet on the circuit of professional events. There is certainly a tendency to feel misunderstood, and sometimes persecuted, by various boards, organizations, state and federal agencies, and also by accrediting associations. Not all their complaints are valid, of course, but there is a very real feeling that the smaller junior colleges do not receive equitable treatment in the accrediting process.

Smaller junior colleges often lack the services of an institutional research specialist, and hence may not have on-going institutional studies of the level of sophistication now being stressed by accrediting bodies. Thus they are hampered in producing the self-study document from existing data and the accumulation of evaluational research and outcomes assessment which is currently receiving emphasis in the rationale of regional accrediting associations. Further, this lack of a well-developed, continuing program of research is a handicap in the long-range planning expected of institutions. The need for planning is evident in all types and sizes of institutions, but the level of sophistication of documentation varies.

Of concern to some is what they believe to be a disproportionately low number of visiting evaluators from smaller, rural institutions, and an alleged disregard for the disparity of background of the visiting evaluators sent to smaller junior colleges. A serious, although unsubstantiated, charge is that smaller institutions receive a disproportionate share of the short review cycles which are handed down by accrediting bodies. Some suggest that there is an assumed quality and accreditability of larger junior colleges, senior colleges, and graduate universities, whereas a "prove thyself" attitude is encountered by the smaller junior colleges.

The Task Force fashioned the principle that although qualitative accreditation is a common concern for institutions of all types and sizes, and thus may involve judgments and input from all sectors, the preponderance of weight in these judgments should rest with representatives from peer institutions. It is recommended that a majority of representatives from small, rural colleges should be included on the accreditation teams visiting such institutions. It seems only fair that this should be the case.

CONCLUSION

This is the environment of service for the majority of two-year college presidents across the land. In spite of the work of the task force, and the subsequent commission, those who labor in this segment continue to do so largely without recognition. Nevertheless, these institutions remain as the grass roots of the community college movement.

Topics for Discussion or Further Study

1. How may one define small/rural as a term applicable to a category of junior colleges?

2. How would you compare the attention given to urban problems and urban institutions in the professional literature and the public media as versus that given to the rural sector and its community colleges?

3. In your opinion, why is this book written from the small/rural perspective, while addressing many concerns of interest to all sectors and tiers of higher education?

4. What are the distinguishing differences in the cultural and the institutional professional environments of the rural and the urban community colleges?

5. How is equal opportunity associated with support of varied components of a community college system, rural and urban?

PERQUISITES
OF THE PRESIDENCY

12

The perquisites, or "perks" as they are sometimes called, of the presidency are discussed more openly in recent times than they once were. For decades these were kept in the closet between boards and presidents, although whispered among faculty and other staff. Revelations in popular literature and other media of the perquisites associated with management in business and industry, along with sunshine laws on public business, have brought these out in the open for general discussion. Fortunately for presidents, there is somewhat better public understanding and acceptance of perquisites than before, although this is not universal by any means.

There will likely continue to be some controversy over perquisites for public officials of all types and at all levels. Just as there is an occasional journalistic or editorial critique, sometimes termed an expose', of perquisites such as limousines for federal officials or a governor's mansion expense, so will some of the perquisites of college and university officials continue to receive unfavorable attention in the media. Tax agencies have begun to look toward placing liability on these as well.

Perquisites should have their basis in the nature of the position and its demands upon the occupant. The presidency makes a demand for an inordinate time obligation, and benefits which might be termed perquisites are often nothing more than services which free the president to perform more valuable functions for the college. In a similar vein, the president should not have to pay expenses for the conduct of college business, or the social obligations of the office, from the taxable salary paid to him for his work.

Several research studies have been done on the perquisites or fringes associated with the presidency. These reveal a wide variation in practices across the nation, some related to institutional type. Generally speaking, junior college presidents have the same general obligations as do university presidents, and the perquisites due to a president cross the lines in higher education.

Unless there are board members present who are familiar with the perquisites of managers in banks and other businesses, there may be some lack of understanding as to what should be promised a new president or provided for a continuing president. Presidents and candidates for president are in an awkward position in attempting to inform and educate boards on this topic, since they may appear to be self-serving. It is with this in mind that this chapter on perquisites has been written (with a disclaimer regarding shifting tax rules and constraining legalities in given situations).

HOUSING

One of the more common perquisites associated with the presidency is the president's home. The president's home should be on the campus itself, preferably situated in an area with some degree of privacy. It is understood that this suggestion may be unrealistic in certain urban settings, but it tends to be applicable in most situations.

If the president is to give the time commitment required to meet the challenges of leadership, he should be freed of the normal, time-consuming problems of home ownership. He should be provided a home with maintenance, security, lawn services, utilities, and other necessities. The home should be large enough, and specially designed, to accommodate the entertainment obligations of the president, as well as his family needs. It should be recognized by campus constituencies and community people as an extension of the president's office, providing therein a study/library to receive visitors on official business.

Of course, it would be a financial hardship for the president to maintain a private residence of his own which would meet these requirements satisfactorily. Further, as presidents change, each new one would face the problems of finding such a facility, and each leaving president would face the problems of disposing of property which has been especially designed for college purposes.

There are several reasons for locating the president's home on campus. One of these is to assure the tax exemption which recognizes location, the office, telephone connections with the college system, and college business functions as relevant. The board must also be on record as requiring that the president occupy the designated residence. Since a college vehicle parked in the home garage has not left the campus, this is relevant to tax rules as well.

The public is likely to perceive the need for a campus home and its utilitarian value, when they would be less likely to perceive such a need if it were located elsewhere. The president is available twenty-four hours a day on campus as emergencies or special needs arise. He can monitor campus functions more effectively. His working office is convenient, and he is close for college activities of all kinds. Maintenance services are more readily available, and less likely to attract adverse comment.

In circumstances where a campus home is not available for the president, the board may provide a housing allowance to assist in offsetting expenses. While susceptible to unfavorable tax rulings, and requiring the keeping of records in some detail if this source of income is to be deductible, the payment of a housing allowance is appropriate when a campus home is not provided. This housing allowance provides a source of funds which assists the president with the added expense of occupying a home which goes beyond the requirements of family, and is sufficient to fulfill the social and business activity needs associated with the position.

In some instances, the housing allowance is used for entertainment and similar expenses, although this tends to overlap with provisions of other expense accounts. This depends somewhat on the total spectrum of perquisites which is being provided. It should be remembered that this allowance is primarily for the purpose of providing a residence suitable for the obligations of the president.

There is some question as to the size of the housing allowance when such is provided in lieu of college housing. As a general rule this should be in an amount to about two-thirds of the cost of rental of a similar home, or a similar proportion of the cost of debt payments on a home of like size and quality with a minimum down payment. To the extent that this payment can be tax-sheltered, it is appropriate to do so.

AUTOMOBILE

The college should provide an automobile for the exclusive use of the president. Most presidents are on the highway quite often, and most find themselves moving about the campus and the community several times a day tending to college affairs. These expenses should not be borne personally, nor should the president be constantly submitting mileage claims, which may or not pay the costs of maintaining and using a car.

While good judgment must be used in the selection of a college car for the use of the president, this vehicle should be a full-sized one of an upper-intermediate quality grade. Since the president frequently takes others on trips with him, size is of some importance. The status of the office, and safety on the highway, suggest a larger, heavier automobile of better quality. However, presidents and boards are wise to avoid purchasing expensive, luxury cars. These bring forth too many criticisms from staff and community.

Again, tax liability may be a problem. If the president uses the automobile for college business only, and if he does not drive it to a home off the campus itself, then this limits such problems.

Every board and every president should examine carefully the officially adopted description of position for the office of president. It is important that this be rather broad and sweeping in its scope. It could be significant that this job description state specifically that the presidency is considered of an around-the-clock nature, and that the president is considered to be a representative of the college in all of his civic and social contacts and endeavors. This subsumes his driving time as related to duties and offers some protection for the president in matters of legal liability at the wheel. It may also assist in arguments over taxes.

Some boards and some presidents prefer to utilize a car allowance versus furnishing a college car. This has some advantage in that it avoids legal requirements of marking and tagging, and it makes the vehicle technically free for personal use. However, it creates some further problems with tax liability, and it is necessary for the president to keep a log of all business use in order to have part or all of the allowance as tax deductible. The president must also bear the expenses and inconveniences of ownership, service, and supplies.

If an automobile allowance is provided, it should be sufficient to meet the demands and expenses of ownership and travel for the usual mileage driven in connection with duties. If the mileage figure is used, and a figure of 20,000 annual miles comes to mind, then this should be multiplied by the maximum per mile reimbursement allowed by the IRS. The allowance should be somewhat greater than this product, since most estimates of the costs of car ownership exceed mileage reimbursement rates. Another approach would be to pay an amount equal to leasing costs of the auto plus about half or more of the allowable figure for mileage by the IRS. Neither of these methods is likely to be as satisfactory as having the automobile furnished by the college, however.

UNRESTRICTED EXPENSE ALLOWANCE

The president has frequent out-of-pocket expenses which accrue to him by virtue of office, i.e. expenses which he might not have as a faculty member or staff member. These are many and varied. He attends many meetings and conventions, the cost of which exceeds travel claim reimbursements. He attends meetings out-of-town for a day and provides his own subsistence. He entertains college guests in town, and he takes others to dinner when he is out-of-town. He donates substantially to any local or campus cause, and buys tickets to fund raisers for local causes. He maintains memberships in private clubs principally for use in entertaining guests or friends of the college. He has social functions in his home at extra expense. He entertains board members and staff on occasion, and he pays for the extras when they travel with him. He must attend certain political and governmental functions where contributions are required. He belongs to civic clubs and the local chamber of commerce and he contributes to their causes.

It is important that the president be given a substantial, unrestricted expense allowance to meet all of these out-of-pocket expenses associated with his position. This should be paid to him monthly in a set amount. Sometimes this is termed a "maintenance allowance," and sometimes it is confused with a housing allowance. However, this is *maintenance* only to the extent that it involves the maintenance of his position. It is instead an unrestricted expense allowance, and is correctly termed so because the board places few, if any, restrictions on how the president may use it. This freedom is essential for the president.

There are some tax concomitants to this expense allowance as well. While the board does not place restrictions on its use, they do require reporting. This may be done annually, and should ordinarily be categorical in nature. However, the president's log book, which he must keep to meet IRS requirements, along with receipts for sums above a prescribed figure, must be open to inspection by the board chairperson or designated member.

Again, the writer must state a disclaimer about offering tax or legal advice, and confine these comments to the general principles which are understood by a layperson. Essentially, the utilization of this fund is at the discretion of the president himself, and the board and institution have no particular tax liability associated with it. The president must use it and account for it as business expenses satisfactory to the IRS, or he must pay taxes on any amounts not properly accounted for under those rules and regulations.

Thus, if the board provides a larger allowance than is needed during a given year, the president has that difference in additional personal income to declare. If the board provides an allowance which is insufficient, then the president must pay some of the expenses associated with his position out of his taxable personal salary income.

For these reasons it is best if the expense allowance is placed at the upper limits of the sum of those out-of-pocket expenses normally incurred. The actual amount may depend somewhat on the circumstances, and the other allowances which are received. However, for the purposes indicated above, a minimum of $500 per month is suggested, ranging upward from that figure if the situation warrants it.

The use of college credit cards is controversial in some locales. There are advantages to so doing when legal restraints allow. In this instance, the charges come directly to the college and are paid from college accounts. While this would cover certain of the expenses cited above, and the expense allowance might be reduced accordingly, it would not cover many of these out-of-pocket expenses. That is to say, use of credit cards would not obviate the need for the expense allowance described. Credit card expenditures are often the subject of scrutiny and controversy, so should be used carefully.

RETIREMENT

The president should have approximately ten percent of his salary set aside into a tax-sheltered, vested, retirement annuity. There are several reasons for this.

Ordinarily, the president will receive whatever retirement benefits accrue to faculty and other employees. In public institutions this will usually be contributions made on behalf of the individual to a state or public employee pension system. Generally this contribution and/or the benefits therefrom will be based on a salary figure with a cap and benefits will be capped as well. This benefit and the social security benefit are likely to be insufficient to provide an adequate retirement program for the president, and perhaps for other higher paid staff as well. Boards have a moral obligation to supplement such benefits for these staff.

The average tenure for presidents is just over five years. This is a high profile position, and one with a high casualty rate. Presidents often move among several different colleges during their career, and these may involve service in different states and under different public retirement systems. Such retirement systems for public employees often require tenure of ten years or more to become vested. Thus, a president could find himself at the time of retirement qualifying for no guaranteed benefits or very limited benefits.

Because the presidency is a high risk position, sometimes presidents find themselves at age fifty-five or so at a disadvantage in the job market and unable to find a position with the remuneration of a presidency. Because the presidency is a high stress position, presidents sometimes find themselves with health problems well before normal retirement age. As a result of these health conditions, they may no longer continue the pace of the presidency, and must search for less demanding professional work at a lower salary level. In either case, retirement benefits will reflect this lower income level during the last five or ten years of their career, even if they continue to participate in the same public employee retirement program.

For the above reasons, it is suggested that boards have an obligation to fund on a pay-as-incurred basis a supplemental retirement program for the president during the time he serves their institution in that high office. A rate of ten percent has been suggested. This is a common rate, and mathematically it appears to be sound. Over a period of twenty years in the presidency it would provide two times annual salary plus accrued interest, which should provide at age sixty-five an income in excess of thirty percent of average salary. Depending on relevant ages, inflation, and interest rates, this could be a helpful supplement.

Boards would be wise to gain the services of a consultant who sets up special pension programs, or they may simply go to the pension and annuity staff of a major insurance company for these services. It appeared recently that there might be federal intervention into this area, but that is forestalled as of the date of this writing. However, use of expert assistance is recommended so as to avoid any anticipated tax or other problems for the college or the individual.

As alluded earlier, it would be appropriate that a similar benefit be provided for other higher paid college employees. Generally speaking, if the total retirement benefits for an employee will not reach at least sixty percent of current salary under the applicable public systems, the board should consider a supplementary program.

OTHER CONSIDERATIONS

It is understood that the president should be eligible for the other benefits which may be extended to professional employees. Presumably these would include term life insurance for one to two times annual salary, health insurance, long-term disability insurance, and the like. Benefits may also include tuition waivers for family and access to special programs.

Some institutions provide ordinary life insurance or limited pay plans for presidents which have accumulating cash values. These are, of course, a desirable benefit, although there may be a tax liability associated with most of them.

It is an advantage to employees, including the president, to provide desired benefit services on a tax-sheltered basis wherever feasible. However, one must stress desired benefits. The tax-sheltered program is a major institutional cost, and it is usually paid from the same sources from which salaries come. The benefits program should purchase only those services which the vast majority of the staff would like to purchase for themselves with their own money, while doing so at a tax savings and perhaps at a cheaper price through group purchasing and bidding.

It is important that any perquisites being provided to the president be a part of the official record of the board and the initial employment letter. These should be clearly stated in the official minutes and in writing to the president, so that there can be no misunderstanding about these at a later time. This also provides substantiation for auditors.

The question of the president's salary is one which frequently perplexes board members. It is, of course, helpful to have the advantage of salary research done within the state and region so that the board will feel comfortable offering the new president compensation which compares favorably with other colleges of like type and size. Salary increases for the continuing president should normally be about the same percentage as those given to other staff who are performing well, although adjustments may be made occasionally to bring the salary in line with comparable institutions or to recognize special merit. As rules of thumb, in small to medium colleges the president's salary should normally be nearly twice that of a faculty member with the same credentials, and about one-third higher than that of the nearest vice president or other administrator.

The board should provide a budget for appropriate professional development activities for the president. These include the attendance at the appropriate annual meetings at the national and regional levels and of certain accrediting bodies. The board should provide for attendance at an occasional summer retreat for the president (and family, if legally permissible).

However, a word of caution must be inserted in regard to the president's presence on campus. Travel and meeting attendance may easily become so excessive as to handicap the accomplishment of important campus work and incur criticisms related to lack of availability. There are so many organized professional groups, and so many meetings which appear to be worthwhile, that presidents could be constantly on the road. It is important that neither professional development, business affairs, nor public relations activities take the president away from his campus obligations an excessive amount of time.

CONCLUSION

There have been few authoritative sources which provide information about the extras associated with the presidency. Certain surveys have been alluded to, and these tend to offer support as to what is customary. There has been a paucity of literature offering a supportive rationale for these perquisites. The presidency is different from other positions in higher education, and it must be understood that the position merits certain added considerations. This chapter has been an effort to explain the perquisites which are customary, appropriate, and deserved, and an attempt to offer reasons why these are essential to success in that office and to fairness for its occupant.

Topics for Discussion or Further Study

1. Are presidential "perks" really fair and/or necessary? Make a case for these, and make a case against them.

2. Should perquisites be negotiated with each new president, or should these be established in board policy and applied to each new occupant of the office? Why?

3. Should the president's salary be twice that of a faculty member as suggested? Take a position and defend it.

4. Describe ways in which the president's home is used as a quasi-official campus facility. Does the official residence constitute more of a fringe benefit than a liability? Take a position and defend it.

EVALUATING
THE PRESIDENT

13

The subject of evaluation of the president is one of some controversy among those who study, write, teach, or practice in related professional positions throughout higher education. There is some evidence of increasing demand from the rank and file faculty and from those second and third echelon administrators, who are subject to some form of evaluation, for a formal evaluation process for the titular leader of the institution and for some meaningful role in that evaluation. Similarly, boards of regents are being led to believe that in order to fulfill their accountability function there must be some sort of formal evaluation of their chief executive officer.

In spite of these expressed interests, the evaluation of presidents continues to be a controversial subject, particularly among practicing presidents. It is one thing to suggest that such a process is appropriate and another to devise an appropriate and fair method in which to conduct the process. Further, it is yet to be established whether such a process may be more harmful than productive, and whether an evaluation may actually interfere with the effective performance of the president.

Kaufmann (1980) takes the position that evaluation is a necessary evil, the potentially harmful effects of which should be minimized at all costs, and that some form of evaluation for presidents is a growing trend and will soon become inevitable. The task then becomes the definition and delineation of a suitable process.

EVALUATION ISSUES

Presumably the evaluation of presidents has some specific purpose or set of purposes. The most suitable and the normal professional purpose of evaluations is that of providing information for guiding the self-development and improvement process of the individual undergoing scrutiny. Any other purpose may be suspect, at least from the standpoint of the subject of the evaluation. The president should not be subjected to the procedure in order to allow faculty, students, or subordinates to take their return shot at him as a morale boosting factor. Neither should the evaluation process be seen as an opportunity for a board to obtain supposedly objective material to use in justifying the discipline or termination of a president who has rankled the membership in personal interchanges and in other ways, nor is it appropriate as an evidence gathering procedure against a president who has shown himself to be inept in obvious ways.

Kaufmann raises several key questions concerning the decision to implement presidential evaluations. Does the evaluation process help to attract and retain presidents of the highest quality? Does it help improve their performance, their productivity, and their job satisfaction? Does it aid in the retention of good presidents and the weeding out of those who are not suitable? Is it regarded as legitimate by those who are affected by it? Such questions sound a warning that these evaluation procedures require careful study prior to implementation. Further, a board which undertakes evaluation with the thought of reminding the president who is the employer and who is the employee may be misusing the process.

Will the evaluation process really assist the board in making a fair assessment of presidential performance? Is it the president who is being evaluated or the board itself? The president is the executive officer of the board in carrying out policy. Regardless of any efforts which might or might not be made by the president to distinguish those acts which are made in the carrying out of policy requirements from those acts which are at his own volition and discretion, these differences are likely to be overlooked in the perceptions of internal constituencies. Thus, the president may receive bad marks (or good marks) as a result of the board policies which he executes. Similarly, judgments of internal groups may well be influenced by the president's enforcement of various objectionable state or governmental regulations promulgated by legislative bodies or bureaucrats.

Any board should consider carefully what characteristics it wants in a president, and to include these in both its hiring and its evaluation practices. If the board wants internal institutional harmony at any cost, this should be clear in the employment of its president. If it wants a well-organized, appropriately structured institution with performance accountability throughout, then the board needs to reflect this in its evaluation practices. The president who runs a "tight ship" at the behest of the board, and the various governmental oversight offices, should not be faulted for negative perceptions which accrue internally as a result.

Another issue in presidential evaluation is that of confidentiality. Any evaluation process which is not appropriately confidential throughout is likely to cause far more problems than it can ever compensate for in positives. First of all, the respondents from internal constituencies, if such are involved, must be properly guarded. Further, the outcomes must be carefully shielded and used only as planned by the board. An evaluation which is to be done for public show is a sham, and should be avoided. Likewise, an evaluation which is a candid appraisal of the individual performance of the titular leader must be shielded from any but its intended use in working with the president to improve his competencies.

A president should be evaluated in relation to the powers and authority delegated to the position. If a president must function in an environment, either internally or externally, which limits his ability to lead the institution in a positive way, then this must be taken into account in planning and interpreting any evaluation which is made. If the president is hamstrung by restrictive policies and regulations, he cannot be faulted for lack of creativity and initiative in leadership. If he is granted a maximum of autonomy and freedom within his institution and with its external relationships, then he may be held accountable for these freedoms.

Perhaps the big question is that of who is qualified to evaluate the president. The obvious answer to this question is, "No one." But this is not a sufficient answer. There are various constituency groups which may make a limited contribution from their perspective on the performance of the president. Each will indeed be limited in scope, limited in understanding, and given from an expected bias. Given these conditions, other administrators, division or department chairs, faculty leaders, student leaders, alumni leaders, board members, community leaders, state liaison officers, and others may make a contribution. It is important to understand that each will make this contribution from their own perspective, whatever that may be, and that none has the global perspective necessary to render a valid judgment on the overall performance of the president. Similarly, none is objective or without bias.

AVOIDING PITFALLS

The "do's" and "don'ts" of evaluation could easily fill numerous pages of text. The listing here is very limited, but several will be implied in the discussion which follows.

The board should not attempt to go through the evaluation process on its own. While the board may contribute to the criteria and the process, this must be a joint venture. The president (or presidents) who are to be evaluated must be involved in developing the criteria and planning the procedure. While plans used in other settings may be helpful, none of these should be expected to fit the local circumstances and situation without some adaptation. Developing an evaluation plan can be, and should be, a rather complex process.

For these reasons and others, it is a good idea that the board retain the services of a qualified consultant or consultants to assist in the development and the carrying through of the evaluation process and procedure. The selection of the consultants should have the concurrence of the president or presidents to be evaluated. In order for the consultants to have credibility with the president, it is likely that they will come from the ranks of presidents or former presidents. Certainly, consultants with past experience as presidents are in the best position to assist in devising suitable criteria and interpreting the results of judgments which are made. These are likely to understand the extreme delicacy of the process and to take the necessary steps to minimize the negative impact of the evaluation on the president's continuing leadership and clout within the institution and with its publics.

The consultants should bring to the planning process ideas or listings of criteria for discussion with the board and with the president. After first discerning just what the expectations of the board may be for the entire effort, the consultants must correct any misinterpretations and ethical flaws in devising or adapting criteria and suggested procedures to the conditions of the application circumstance. This joint planning effort is essential to the success of the evaluation focus. The criteria and the procedure need to be generally acceptable to the president, as well as the board, in order for the outcomes to be considered as credible.

It is inappropriate for members of the board to go into the institution or to go personally to representatives of external constituencies to conduct the evaluation. Few would have the time to do so, and few would have the necessary expertise. More damning would be the effects of the presence of board members engaging in these activities. Similarly, it is insufficient and inappropriate to evaluate the president through the mail, or through simple distribution of questionnaires to a sampling of people.

A proper evaluation procedure involves the development of a standard interview form reflecting the criteria developed. Further, the consultants should meet personally, preferably one-on-one, with the preselected respondents to obtain and record expressions and view-points. If this appears to be an involved process, one can only respond that such an important activity as the evaluation of the president cannot best be accomplished by expeditious shortcuts. After administering the standard interviews or questionnaires with representatives of various constituencies, the consultants should then prepare an interpretive report for the board members, retaining the detail in their own confidential files. The report, since it deals with a personnel matter, should also be considered as confidential under most sunshine laws. If not, then the consultants should meet individually with board members and render an oral report.

While the development of criteria and the procedure for conducting the evaluation have been discussed in general terms above, it must be understood that these are essential elements of an evaluation plan. Such a plan will have features other than these, including the naming of the constituencies and the method of selection of representatives for sampling. It should be the role of the consultants to prepare the entire evaluation plan, after appropriate consultation with the board and the president. Any such plan should have the general concurrence of both the agency (board) commissioning the project and the affected party (the president/s) in all of its aspects.

In order to obtain as complete a picture of presidential performance as possible from the perspective of as many relevant constituencies as is reasonable, the writer recommends consideration of the following in the sampling of views; lower echelon administrators, academic unit leaders, faculty leaders and rank and file faculty, student leaders, non-academic office personnel, alumni leaders, community leaders, and liaison agencies or organizations. Not all of these are necessary, of course, and in some circumstances certain groups should be omitted. The format used may need to be adapted somewhat for each different group.

Generally, the respondents should be preselected by virtue of an office held (such as department head), or by a random method in selecting from within a designated grouping. There are reasons why titular leaders should not be the only ones interviewed in certain categories. Sometimes faculty or student titular leadership may be composed of those who are most activist in their style, not necessarily the most productive or rational members of their constituency. These must be counterbalanced by others who are rank and file. In order to assure the president that certain viewpoints will not be omitted from the process, it is recommended that the president be allowed to designate specific persons to be included along with those chosen at random or by virtue of office. While this may be said to bias the sampling, it may also be termed as a measure to ensure fairness in the process. Certainly, this step will make acceptance of the outcomes easier by the person most affected. One of the common fears of presidents is that evaluators will by chance or design see all of the wrong people. No president is universally popular among all the members of any constituency.

Construction of the evaluation instrument is, of course, a critical part of the process. This will be discussed further in the section to follow. It is very important that the items be phrased in a positive way. Standardized interview questions, as well as questionnaires, may be phrased in such a manner that negative responses are likely to be elicited. If feasible, and it is not always feasible, the items should be behavioral in style. Nevertheless, it may be desirable at times and for certain purposes to obtain responses to items which are admittedly tapping strictly subjective perceptions and opinions. When the latter is done, it should be clear to interpreters and users of the data that it is perceptions rather than facts which have been gathered.

The timing of evaluations and their routine scheduling is a matter which deserves some attention and thought. It is unlikely that an annual evaluation of the president is necessary or appropriate. Where the president is elected for a fixed term of years, and contract renewal is eminent, then this may affect the scheduling of the evaluation. Generally speaking, where presidents continue to serve indefinitely at the pleasure of the board, an evaluation every two or three years is sufficient. The evaluations are best scheduled mid-year, probably during the months of November or December but no later than January. This should be completed and in compilation prior to the time when the president becomes involved in the evaluation of subordinates or faculty evaluations begin to occur. Avoid scheduling an evaluation during a period of campus crisis or turmoil, lest it be interpreted in such a manner as to weaken the president's ability to deal with the current problems or result in responses which are emotionally attuned to the conflicts of the moment.

EVALUATION CRITERIA & THE INSTRUMENT

Both Seldin (1988) and Kauffman (1980) provide some information and guidance on the evaluation process, exemplary criteria, and instruments of assessment. Kauffman also cites failures in the implementation of criteria which have every appearance of rationality. Thus, while the development of the criteria, and an instrument which seeks to assess these, is critically important to the evaluation process, the manner of use is equally significant. Indeed, it often appears that there may be more pitfalls than promises in evaluation efforts for which there have been objective critiques.

The development of criteria should follow the lines of the president's job description. In the absence of a suitable or detailed job description, criteria should follow the format of the postulated duties and responsibilities as these are commonly understood among professionals in higher education. Although beset with some past controversy, the Florida system (State University System of Florida) appears to offer a very logically developed set of criteria and an instrument to match. The system employed by the State Colleges of Pennsylvania is similarly impressive, although its application appears to be somewhat negatively toned. While Seldin (1988) concentrates primarily on processes and instruments for the evaluation of administrators other than the president, some of those presented in his work have merit and adaptability.

The outline which follows is intended only as another example of one which might be adapted and extended to fit a given circumstance. The writer is indebted to the writers mentioned above for a several of the ideas contained within the format outlined in the criteria and manifestations listed below.

A. Planning and Priorities
    1. Sets clear priorities and goals for the college.
    2. Articulates goals well orally and in written communications.
    3. Works cooperatively in internal goal development.
    4. Works cooperatively with college governance in goal development.
    5. Maintains a planning process and proper documentation.
    6. Priorities and goals reflect the essential purposes of the college as stated and adopted.
    7. Strives for consensus on goals and objectives.
    8. Sets forth a clear direction for the future of the college.
    9. Demonstrates initiative in goal setting.
    10. Shows foresight and vision in planning efforts.

B. Leadership and Management
    1. Maintains an internal system of dynamics conducive to policy development and change.
    2. Follows regents' policies in administering the college.
    3. Follows state and other regulations in administration.
    4. Maintains a clear internal organizational structure with clear and commonly understood responsibilities.
    5. Maintains an internal system of governance conducive to obtaining input from professional staff.

6. Demonstrates knowledge of collegiate finance and budgeting systems.
7. Provides for opportunities for input into budget needs by professional staff.
8. Delegates budget management responsibilities as necessary.
9. Maintains personal checks on financial operations and status.
10. Keeps governing board informed on financial matters
11. Represents the college effectively in funding competition.
12. Develops and implements funding priorities and strategies within the college.
13. Recognizes and appoints qualified and competent administrators.
14. Coordinates, supervises, and directs the work of administrators effectively.
15. Demonstrates the ability to make decisions
16. Recognizes the significance of timeliness for self and others.
17. Demonstrates knowledge and concern for cost control and productivity.
18. Delegates authority without abdicating presidential responsibilities.
19. Recognizes the significance of each office and facet of administration.
20. Has developed effective teamwork in administration.
21. Remains on campus a sufficient proportion of time to effectively administer the college.
22. Maintains proper personnel office practices and records.
23. Demonstrates knowledge and execution of proper procedures in campus facilities development.
24. Exercises proper fund management to assure solvency of various accounts.
25. Recognizes critical areas of management needing personal attention.
26. Management characterized more by crisis avoidance than crisis intervention.
27. Maintains or sees to the maintenance of a proper institutional records system.

C. Internal Relationships
1. Demonstrates an understanding of the significance of the professional roles of campus personnel.
2. Demonstrates professional courtesies in campus relationships.
3. Exercises strategies for maintaining communications with professional staff.

4. Shows respect for campus governance systems in place and utilizes these appropriately.
5. Demonstrates appropriate concern for academic standards and academic issues.
6. Shows an interest in curriculum and program development efforts.
7. Leads in the development and/or implementation of an enlightenedsystem of personnel policies.
8. Participates appropriately in the selection of new staff with a concern for quality.
9. Is available and receptive to staff.
10. Visits various campus areas and programs periodically.
11. Is generally recognized by students on campus.
12. Demonstrates interest in student activities.
13. Demonstrates interest in student governance.
14. Is receptive to student leaders.
15. Is receptive students with individual problems which have not been resolved elsewhere.
16. Makes frequent appearances at campus activities and events.
17. Personally sets a tone philosophically which stresses concern for student welfare, fairness, and courtesy.
18. Recognizes and respects academic integrity and proper academic practices and traditions.
19. Makes merit decisions based upon a consistent rationale and available information.
20. Respects productivity and accomplishments more than showmanship in recognitions accorded subordinates.
21. Deals evenhandedly with various campus groups and individuals.
22. Encourages directly, or through policies, the professional development of campus staff.
23. Demonstrates assertiveness and firmness when appropriate.
24. Makes definite efforts to keep college constituencies properly informed on issues and problems.
25. Is known for fairness and impartiality in decisions.
26. Demonstrates a consciousness for freedoms as well as controls.
27. Is relatively free of personality attributes which interfere with position effectiveness.
28. Shows charisma in campus leadership.
29. Recognizes the priority of on-campus responsibilities.
30. Demonstrates an appropriate interest in instructional strategies and technology.
31. Is presidential in appearance and style.

D. External relationships
   1. Attempts to promote positive town and gown relationships.
   2. Maintains an effective relationship with state and governmental offices and agencies.
   3. Exercises appropriate strategies in working with news and public media.
   4. Participates and encourages others to participate in area civic improvement groups.
   5. Encourages campus work with alumni organizations.
   6. Encourages and participates in the work of the college foundation and in fund raising activities.
   7. Makes speaking appearances at area meetings and events.
   8. Demonstrates concern for area economic development and cooperates with local strategies and programs.
   9. Actively participates in organizations of presidents seeking improvements in conditions affecting the college.
   10. Participates in national and regional organizations of which the college is a member.
   11. Leads the college in maintaining respectable accreditation status with the regional association and with specialized groups.
   12. Interacts with the governing board in a professional manner.
   13. Exercises strategies for keeping the governing board properly informed on matters within their purview.
   14. Provides leadership in a recommending role for policy development by the governing board.
   15. Represents the college favorably in written and oral communications.
   16. Is presidential in appearance and conduct.

This listing is by no means exhaustive. The criteria and the instruments of evaluation may be almost infinite in their length and comprehensiveness. However, there is likely to be a point of diminishing returns of value in relation to effort in data gathering. Also, there will be increasing overlap as the listing grows. The listing presented above has been almost entirely behavioral or performance oriented. The perception approach and adjectival format would tend to produce a much different listing. Nevertheless, it should be noted that these behavioral items remain subjective in nature and still depend upon individual views and opinions.

The listing above is adaptable to the use of the five-point Likert scale in formatting it as an assessment instrument. Perhaps it would also be appropriate to include a response option outside of the Likert

Scale which might be worded "No basis for judgment." The five Likert responses are:

Almost always
Usually
Occasionally
Seldom
Almost never

It is possible to add open-ended or unstructured questions to the evaluation instrument. These are, of course, difficult to reduce to summary form, and there may be a tendency to over interpret either a single or a few responses, usually of the negative variety, when these are reported in a document. These may provide a release valve for expression from respondents, but their contribution (or harm) to the evaluation effort depends upon the skill of the consultants in interpretation.

CONCLUSION

To evaluate or not to evaluate may not be the question. The evaluation of presidents, as well as other administrator performances, is likely to be a part of the future in institutions of higher education. The question is: How and by whom?

Presidents are not unaccustomed to evaluations. They receive evaluations and critiques almost daily in the faculty coffee lounge and in downtown restaurants and gathering places. They receive occasional evaluation in the student meeting places as well. As alumni gather, an evaluation of some areas of the president's performance is a likely happening. State offices and regulatory agencies are often chagrined by the obstinacy of the president and subordinates in their insistence on maintaining institutional autonomy and freedoms, so they will join with evaluations of their own. It is not necessary to be well informed in order to participate in these informal, on-going evaluations of the president's performance. In fact, information may actually inhibit the free-wheeling style of these sessions. Sometimes even the press contributes by giving a public forum for such evaluations either through its reporting or its letters columns.

The formal evaluation process, such as one based upon the recommendations cited here, will not supplant the informal processes which are occurring, nor is it likely even to diminish the intensity of these. Unless it is properly handled, a formal evaluation may contribute to these unofficial vehicles of evaluation. However, the design and implementation of a formal evaluation process does have the advantage of offering a more structured alternative to the processes described in the foregoing paragraph. Since the governing board is likely to be aware of the general tone and tenor of the informal processes, and at times may give undue credibility to such commentary, it could be helpful to all concerned to have a formal process in place.

However, it must be remembered that the formal process is simply one which gleans opinion on the performance of the president in accordance with the structure of a listed set of criteria and behavioral manifestations as viewed by the respondents. These are then quantified. These continue to remain opinions and judgments of people, not all of whom will disqualify themselves in areas about which they have no direct knowledge. Nevertheless, in spite of its known weaknesses, such an evaluation process is likely to be superior to the rumor and gossip mill product which is its alternative.

Presidents who are faced with increasing pressures for adoption of evaluation plans would be wise to consider these thoughts above. They would also be wise to become involved in the design and development of an evaluational schematic if such looms as a certainty on the horizon. The evaluational activity may prove to be the horror it is feared to be, or it may be turned into one which is minimally disturbing and offers some evidence that the president is seen as performing his duties in a satisfactory and proper manner.

Topics for Discussion or Further Study

1. Assume that you have been assigned the debate question: "Resolved that the evaluation of college presidents is both necessary and inevitable." Take both the affirmative and the negative positions and make cases.

2. Summarize the cautions which should be exercised in planning and conducting presidential evaluations.

3. Can the evaluation of a president ever be fully isolated from influences of the governance system under which he serves? Take a position and defend it.

4. From the listing provided, or from other sources, select and defend seven criteria which you believe to be the most significant in evaluating a president.

PART FOUR

Case Situations

CASE SITUATIONS

14

The following case situations are presented in terse, summary form Some are based upon actual events, with minor modifications, and others are partially or entirely fictional. It is understood that there may be insufficient information given in some instances to determine justifiably correct responses. Therefore, each respondent to a case situation may find it necessary to create further conditions as a part of the response given. If so, this will serve as a part of the exercise. Responses are to be given primarily from the viewpoint of the presidency, although that office may or may not be dealing with the issue directly.

These case situations are presented as learning exercises for students or persons new to community college administration. Further, these may have heuristic value for readers aspiring to presidential leadership or other administrative positions. They are designed to bring learned principles to bear upon specific case situations which demand a response from the person who occupies the office of president.

Case 1 *Faculty Conflict*
The program directors of two areas have had harsh and emotional words over differences in views as to necessary choices and decisions in a project which must be performed cooperatively. Neither person can be readily determined as right or wrong. Both are conscientious, competent, and valuable staff members. Your chief academic officer has had past encounters with each of these persons and may be prejudiced. Each has come to the president's office to complain about the other. How do you handle this situation?

Case 2 *Student Discipline*
A student has admitted to having placed a female undergarment on the college flagpole and raised it during the night. The student personnel dean has taken action to expel the student from college two weeks before the end of the spring semester. The faculty/student disciplinary committee has sustained the dean's action by a split vote.

The student has had only minor disciplinary problems before. The student and his parents admit fault but appeal the harshness of the decision to the president. How do you handle this appeal?

Case 3   *Faculty Conflict*

The chairperson of a struggling program and the most experienced faculty person in that program have lost confidence in one another's professionalism and are personally at odds. They have had words privately and publicly. Both are known to be emotional, and the chairperson is known to be particularly volatile. The faculty member tends to withdraw and has become uncommunicative. The program is one in which some six faculty must function with a high degree of teamwork. Just as the fall term begins, the chairperson enters the president's office and declares that she can no longer work with this faculty member and wants her fired. The faculty member comes in and says she can no longer stand the abuse of the chairperson and wants to quit. This is an area in which potential faculty are extremely scarce, and it would be next to impossible to locate a suitable replacement on short notice. Both know this. Both have a good relationship with the president. How do you handle this situation?

Case 4   *Academic Freedom*

While introducing and presenting students with prepared speeches on a matter of national policy and legislation at a civic club program, a faculty member meanders to discuss national policy himself, presenting a very one-sided viewpoint. In the course of this, the faculty member refers to certain liberal Democrat members of the Congress as "communist-pinko." You are there. This is offensive to businesspersons of that political persuasion, and they tell you so. This is a faculty member who is ordinarily circumspect, competent, and well-liked on campus. He assumes and declares this to be a part of academic freedom. How do you handle this?

Case 5   *Sexual Harassment*

A married faculty member in his early thirties is reported by two female students to the academic dean as inviting them separately to his office and making suggestive remarks and overtures for dates. This is a non-tenured faculty member who shows academic promise, but he is in his first year at the college. He confides with the dean that he and his wife have been having problems. The dean confers with you as to the appropriate action. What is your advice?

Case 6 *Instructor "Cursing"*

A female student comes to the president's office after having already been to the academic and student personnel deans. She complains that one male instructor is cursing in class, that it is offensive to her and another student, and that she has been unable to get other college officials to take any action. She tells you that she is quite religious and that this language bothers her. You ask her to tell you exactly what words this faculty member is using. Reluctantly, she tells you, "hell" and "damn." What is your response to this? Do you follow up in any way?

Case 7 *Flag Desecration*

Two students come to the president's office complaining that the American flag is being desecrated by clothing being sold in the college bookstore. The dean of student affairs has referred them to your office with their complaint. They state their concerns with patriotism and that stars and stripes material is appearing on the seat of shorts sold. They believe this to be a breach of flag etiquette. How do you handle this?

Case 8 *Magazine in the Bookstore*

Unknown to you as president or to any other college administrative officer, the person in charge of the college bookstore has added *a* sexually explicit magazine to the others being sold. The first you hear of this is when a delegation of three students come to your office to complain about this "vulgar trash" being sold on campus to students. How do you handle this?

Case 9 *Indecent Literature*

A businessman and his wife who attend your church approach you in the church parking lot asking if you know that there is indecent literature in the library, and that an excerpt from a book by this same atheistic writer is being used in the literature anthology for English classes. You admit not knowing this, and you ask what particular selection they regard as indecent. They give you a title which you recognize as being written by Ernest Hemingway. In the course of conversation you discover that these people are members of the John Birch Society, and that a publication of that organization is their basis for describing the piece as offensive. How do you respond?

Case 10 *Spelling Requirement*

You learn from counselors and faculty advisors who complain that the English faculty are including spelling in their basic course of study for freshman English for three weeks, and that numerous students are failing the course as a result of a spelling test required. The academic dean is aware of this and accepts it reluctantly. You ask the chairperson if this is true, and you are told that spelling is indeed covered and a test given but no one fails for that reason alone. Complaints continue, so you ask questions of English faculty members. They tell you that the spelling test is given and that anyone who does not spell 90 of the 100 words taken from the listing of 1,000 most commonly misspelled words cannot pass the course. This is a rule of the department, they say. How do you approach this problem? Or, is it a problem?

Case 11 *Dating Student*

A non-tenured instructor in psychology, whose services have been generally satisfactory, has been counseling an adult single mother in his class on family problems. He begins to stop by her apartment on his morning fitness jog. Others, including his wife, become aware of his extra attentions to this student. The student tells friends, who tell faculty and others, that he is coming to see her regularly at odd hours. The wife moves the man out, and he begins to live with the student. This is a small college in a small town. Complaints come from all directions that he is unfit to teach. Is this personal affair any business of the college administration? If so, how should it be approached?

Case 12 *Credit for Faculty Member*

A valued faculty member needs either proficiency or credit in a foreign language to qualify for an advanced degree at a university. She arranges, with the academic dean's approval, to take the two courses in a foreign language with a colleague by independent study. She makes an "A" in the first course, but does not complete the requirements for the second course until summer, at which time the colleague has left the state. The new instructor is offended by being asked to evaluate her performance by the registrar and will not do so. Somewhat knowledgeable of the language, the dean does an evaluation, checks it with a proficient friend, and orders the registrar to enter a grade so that the faculty member can go ahead with graduation from the university. The registrar refuses, and the dean enters a grade in the record and signs for it. The registrar files a complaint with the president, claiming that it is improper for the dean to enter a grade. You are aware of some past friction between the dean and the registrar. How do you handle this?

Case 13 *Athlete Loses Scholarship*

An athlete has had a full-scholarship during the past semester. He returns the following fall semester and "goes out" for the sport with others at the proper time. After two weeks the coach dismisses him from the team and pulls his scholarship for "attitude" problems. The student appeal is referred by the athletic director to the president's office. You want to be fair with the student, who may now have to drop out of college, but you are reluctant to force the coach to take a player he considers disruptive and does not want. What do you do?

Case 14 *Liquor Bottle*

You are accompanying students on a long bus ride to an athletic tournament, although you are not their sponsor. You are sitting near the front as you arrive at a motel. As students depart the bus, the student government leader, a pleasant, fun-loving young man and a positive campus leader, drops a liquor bottle which had been concealed in his coat. The bottle lands at your feet. This is against college rules. What do you do at this time? What do you do later?

Case 15 *Plotting Food Fight*

Two student government leaders are accused by an assistant dean of students of plotting a food fight in the college cafeteria to protest the unsatisfactory quality of food being served by the catering contractor. He puts both on disciplinary probation, which means they can no longer head the student government. He asked your advice but has not followed it. In investigating the matter yourself, you find that the catering manager and the assistant dean are "buddies." Also, you conduct an unannounced visit to the cafeteria and find the food deplorable. What do you do?

Case 16 *Manner of Address*

As a new president, it is your desire to maintain a somewhat formal image on campus, thinking that the office of president is one of some dignity which you should uphold in your conduct and dress. However, you try also to appear open and friendly with staff. Most persons recognize your intentions and refer to you as "Doctor." However, a few staff will refer to you as "Doc" and two call you "boss." One or two administrators will call you by your first name in private. A faculty member asks you in a meeting just how you want to be addressed. How do you answer?

Case 17 *Student Questions*

You are invited by the sponsor of a student organization to appear and answer questions regarding the general conduct of your office so that they might better understand the workings of the college. You request a list of questions in advance. One of these questions is: "What are the limits of your power?" How do you answer this?

Case 18 *Letter to the Editor*

It has become necessary in your opinion, and in the opinions of the department chairperson and the academic dean, not to reemploy a non-tenured faculty member for another year. One element of the cause, but not the sole reason, involves this person's behavior which could be embarrassing to the college. There are other causes relating to lax academic standards and course requirements. Policies do not require the formal statement of reasons, and this has not been done. A group of three student favorites of this faculty person come to see you, and receiving no reply to their satisfaction proceed to publish an uncomplimentary letter in a local newspaper. What do you do, if anything?

Case 19 *Governance Issue*

Statutes specifically empower the college governing boards to employ and set compensation of staff. However, the state coordinating board is given the authority to approve budgets for the purpose of setting these in the state finance office for expenditure. In response to wishes of legislative leaders and others in government, the state board directs all colleges to give average raises of a stated percentage and to provide individual raises on the basis of merit. They require a report on compliance to accompany the budget when it is filed for approval. What should be the response of college governing boards and presidents? Do you lodge objections even if others do not?

Case 20 *Board Relations*

It is the custom of your board to rotate chairpersons. One of the members, who is known to be more activist than others, becomes chair. Prior to his first meeting as chair, he calls other board members and invites them to meet with him informally in another city to discuss college affairs. At this time, there is no "sunshine law" forbidding this. You find out from another board member that this is occurring. What is your course of action?

Case 21 *Local Government Relations*

Without prior announcement or discussion, the local city council meets and votes to raise utility rates. The college is the only consumer in its class, and its rates are tripled. Some increase is probably justified, but this is during the second month of a new budget year and will cause hardship. The city must depend on the college's cooperation in certain ways or suffer hardships of its own on other matters. You learn first about the rate increase by reading the local newspaper. How do you approach this problem?

Case 22 *Selection Interview*

You are a candidate for a position as president, and you have been fortunate enough to be selected as a finalist for interviews on campus. You are the guest of a group of a dozen or so faculty who are quizzing you on various issues. You are asked your views about the use of student evaluations, about expectations for campus time commitments of faculty, and about expectations for faculty dress and grooming. You have definite ideas about these matters, but you believe that these may not be popular with a few of those listening. You are not sure about others. How do you answer?

Case 23 *Faculty Privileges*

You are a new president. Upon arrival and settling into the position, you have been approached by various faculty persons who have been frustrated in some way by the views, actions, or inactions of the past president. They are hoping for changes which will please them. One of the issues raised is that of privileged parking in the center of the campus for faculty members. You know that reserving this area would invite student resentment and complaints. However, you know also that this would be a well-received action by most faculty. What do you do?

Case 24 *Academic Assignment*

A tenured and valued faculty member comes to the president's office very upset. She has just been told by the department chair and the academic dean that her favorite course will be taken from her teaching assignment for the ensuing semester and given to a less qualified faculty member with a different specialty in order to give this other person a more complete teaching load. This instructor believes this to be unfair, academically inappropriate and unsound. She appeals this action and requests reversal. What do you do?

Case 25 *Student Grade Appeal*

A student and his parents come to the president's office to lodge an appeal of a course grade. The college has an appeals procedure which requires students first to visit with the instructor and the department head before going to the dean. He has done this. A visit with the dean reveals that there is no difference of opinion about the grades made on tests and assignments, and that he (the dean) believes the averaging was wrong and that the student is right. The matter is referred to a faculty appeals committee which rules in favor of the instructor. The student and his parents appeal again to the president. Upon questioning two members of the appeals committee, it is found that the basis for their ruling is a statement made by the instructor orally in class as to how averaging would be done. This oral statement is in conflict with the official course syllabus on file in the dean's office. According to the statement on averaging in the syllabus, the student obviously deserves a higher grade. What do you do?

Case 26 *Workshop Speaker*

A motivational speaker brought in by the dean to conduct a faculty workshop presents ideas on grading system which you as president believe to be highly experimental at best, and at worst detrimental to the academic standards of the institution. Further, it promises to be a nightmare in academic record-keeping. Several faculty members are quite sold on these ideas as educational innovations. They begin practicing these methods, much to the chagrin of other faculty who are more traditional. The academic dean does not want to stifle creativity and innovation. Faculty and student delegations come to the president expressing concern for standards and requesting his intervention. The governing board has heard something of these ideas, and certain members have put the president on the spot as to whether he can defend the practices. You believe that there are legitimate academic standards issues involved. What do you do in this situation?

Case 27 *Journalism Facts*

Several faculty program leaders with student organizations active in their area and several administrators come to the president's office separately complaining about news stories in the college press. The faculty supervisor of the college newspaper also teaches the journalism classes. These complaints center upon student reporters who write critical stories about activities initiated by these faculty and administrators without checking either the facts involved or asking for explanations from their offices. They believe that the student body is being misled by faulty and unfair reporting, and they request the president to intervene. What do you do?

Case 28 *Problem Secretary*

The secretary to one of the other administrators is reported to be a problem. These reports come from faculty, administrators, and other secretaries, but not from the administrator in charge. Your own observations of the behavior of this secretary tend to confirm reports. She is difficult for other secretaries to work with, and some good people are threatening to quit. Also, she has been unable to find material in her files, and correspondence which she has produced has been brought to you for examination. It is faulty in quality and not representative of standards expected for the college. After twice mentioning these problems to the administrator in charge, she has done nothing to improve the situation nor has she recommended discharge. You are convinced that the secretary needs to go. What do you do?

Case 29 *Academic Freedom*

A non-tenured business instructor, who has already received some criticism in evaluations, is creating some controversy by reportedly teaching unethical business practices in class, explaining how these are done, saying that he has done some, and apparently speaking favorably about these unethical and/or illegal practices. These reports come from off-campus businesses and bankers, from adult students on campus, and from departmental colleagues. The department chair has confronted the instructor about this, and the instructor admits he has done so. He claims that this is a part of his academic freedom. The chair brings this information to the academic dean and the president jointly. How do you advise handling the matter?

Case 30 *Ethnic Jokes*

A. It has been reported quietly that a lower level administrator in his first year at the college is telling ethnic jokes at a table in the faculty lounge. As president you notice a sudden quietness at times when you enter the room, and once or twice you have overheard some bits and pieces of his conversations which lead you to believe that these are true reports. The reports indicate that some are offended by these ethnic jokes, but laughs appear to indicate that others may not be offended at all. What is there about this situation that should concern you? How do you handle it?

B. Consider this same case situation with a slight change of scenario. The administrator is telling jokes with sexual innuendo and some with crude or vulgar content. Female staff members at an adjoining table overhear these, are offended, and report these to their supervisors, who send them to see the president. Do you handle this any differently than the case above? Why, or why not?

Case 31 *Failing Students*

You are a president in your second year in office. Upon examining institutional research on faculty grading practices, you note that for the last two semesters one tenured English instructor has failed 30% and 35% of his classes in basic English and has awarded no "A" grades. This is considerably different than the marks given by colleagues, who have similar class groups. The lowest students on the screening test were siphoned off earlier into developmental classes. The academic dean agrees that there is a problem, and wants your advice on how to approach it. What do you tell him?

Case 32 *Academic Standards*

You note from institutional research data that the average composite test score of entering freshmen falls at the 35th percentile nationally. However, you note also that the average grade point of freshmen at the college is 2.9, which is a "B" average. Should this be of any concern to you as president? If so, how do you approach this apparent discrepancy?

Case 33 *Audit Recommendation*

The college auditing firm has completed its annual audit, which includes recommendations on internal controls. Auditors want better controls in accounting for incoming orders of supplies and equipment. In their report they recommend that the college maintenance facility, located two blocks from the center of campus, be the receiving center for all orders, that these be opened there, and counts be made in comparison with purchase orders. The maintenance facility is a large open area, a hub of activity, and subject to wind and dust. Staff are concerned about security, loss, damage, and handling of delicate materials in this environment. The college can ill afford to separate an area with added staffing to do this. You prefer past practices to continue, which involves delivery to maintenance and redirect to the departments who open packages and check invoices against purchase orders. Is there a possibility of collusion in the past practice? How do you respond to this recommendation?

Case 34 *Federal Privacy Act*

As president you receive a telephone call from a president in a community college in another state. He is very angry and wants to know how your academic records on a basketball player now at his college got into the hands of a coach at a competing college in that state. He wants to know if no one ever heard of the federal privacy law. You tell him that you do not know how this happened, but you intend to find out. It turns out that one of your newer, non-tenured instructors is a friend of that coach in the competing school, and that he has gone to the registrar's office and obtained from the clerk the academic records on the athlete when he was at your college. He has mailed these to his friend, who then contested the NJCAA eligibility of the player successfully. You are appalled at this scenario. What do you do?

Case 35 *Work Conflict*

You are in your first year as president. The professional environment of the college has been somewhat lax, as indicated by accrediting reports as well as personal observations. Just after lunch you and another administrator are driving down a road on business and notice one of the long-tenured faculty on a tractor plowing the field of his farm. College policies require office hours and time on campus which would preclude a faculty member taking afternoons indiscriminately for personal business. Upon asking questions, you find that this practice has been customary with this particular instructor for several years. What do you do?

Case 36 *Entrepreneur*

One of your valued faculty members has been teaching a popular activity course for adults as a part of the college community service curricular program, but now declines to do so again. Instead, this faculty member decides to go into business on his own and offers to conduct the activity for regulars in college facilities and collect a reduced charge personally. He can make more money this way than by accepting the extra pay from the college for doing it, and this pleases participants because their cost is less. How do you respond to this news from your community services director? What if the proposed instruction had been off-campus?

Case 37 *Golf Players*

In order to carry the evening course and extension classes, several instructors are teaching these courses as overloads for extra compensation. Two of these have been taking an afternoon off each week playing golf at the local course. As president you receive complaints from local business people about public employees playing during the work day. The staff members involved believe that because of their extra night duties they are entitled to these afternoons off. What position do you take? Would your position be different if the night courses had been taught as a part of regular loads?

Case 38 *Racial Bias*

After first visiting with a counselor, a sophomore minority student is referred directly to your office (although there is another procedure) complaining about racial bias in the grading practices of a non-tenured faculty member. This is the first such complaint against this person, but it is also the first such complaint by this student. The student states that she believes all of her other instructors to have been fair over the past year and a half. How seriously do you take this complaint? How do you handle it? Would you approach it differently if the student were a freshman and had levelled complaints against several experienced instructors?

Case 39 *Minority Politics*

The college's special counselor for Native American students, a very academic and a socially and politically sensitive individual, has begun to take sides with certain tribal factions on issues in opposition to established tribal leaders. The college's advisory committee on Indian student affairs is made up of designees of tribal chairpersons, and tribal officials have been helpful in maintaining special funding subsidies for this counseling program. Some tribal officials complain to the president about the tribal political activities of this counselor, threatening to withdraw support. How do you handle this problem? Would this issue be different and be approached differently if the constituent groups were the Urban League and the NAACP?

Case 40 *Active Spouse*

Your spouse is a very competent, energetic person who takes an active interest in college affairs and whose interests have been in campus aesthetics, in social functions, and in coordinating special campus events and general activities. As a result, your spouse comes into contact with professional and other staff personnel in a supervisory role. Staff begin to complain increasingly about being "bossed" by the president's spouse, and speak disparagingly of the "Other President." You are advised by an off-campus friend that this is occurring, and that it may be hurting your leadership as president. What is your response to this criticism?

Case 41 *Vendor Favors*

A. You notice that on occasion some lower echelon administrators and some division chairpersons are entertained for lunch by representatives of vendors doing business with the college. You have heard that these individuals (and their spouses) are entertained on a night out in a major city at times. In a few instances you have reason to believe that certain vendors are being favored over others in the phrasing of bid specifications, or in direct ordering where policies and regulations permit. What should be your policy on this, and how do you approach the issue?

B. You find that the bookstore manager (or food services manager) will occasionally order from companies which give a premium gift as an inducement. You question whether these companies are being favored, even at higher prices. What do you about this?

C. You hear that one vendor who sells supplies to the college has given the division head's spouse an expensive present. What is your position, and how do you handle the situation?

D. It is during the bidding period for some rather expensive equipment. Privately, without witnesses, vendors make you the following offers. How do you handle each of these?

1. A cash bribe.
2. A trip to a resort for you and your spouse.
3. A large contribution to the college's student scholarship fund.

Case 42 *Faculty Fraternizing*

As president you have encouraged a friendly and familial atmosphere on campus. However, you have noted that two married faculty members of opposite sex are extremely friendly and familiar. They have become a focal point of the staff gossip mill, and even students are discussing and joking about this close relationship. You have no knowledge that anything improper is occurring, but appearances suggest that it might be. Do you consider this simply a personal matter, or is this a legitimate interest of the administration?

Case 43 *Evaluation of the President*

One of your board members has been to a national meeting for community college trustees. One session was on the topic of evaluation of presidents. She comes home inspired and during a meeting expounds on what she has heard. This sounds good to several other members. They suggest that a trustee committee make up a questionnaire to be given to all faculty and subordinate administrators asking them to rate the president. How do you respond to this situation?

Case 44 *Faculty Evaluation System Study*

An academic dean with long tenure comes to you with information that the faculty committee wishes to make a study of all of the faculty evaluation systems in vogue in a number of area junior colleges. Both you and the dean have visited many other colleges on accrediting evaluations and looked at evaluation systems. Also, you are both aware that several other area colleges have patterned their systems after the one pioneered in your own college. The dean has

served as a consultant to some of these colleges on the topic. Your
system is considered to be "state of the art." You suspect faculty might
like something less rigorous and comprehensive. Your dean is the
"parent" of the system. What is your advice on this matter?

Case 45 *Minority Faculty Leaving*

A young, black, male faculty member comes to you to discuss
professional career planning. You have taken a personal interest in
this man since he was a student at your college and was employed by
you as soon as he completed a master's degree. You have mentored
him, and he and his wife regard you highly. He is thinking of taking a
subordinate university position so that he can complete a doctorate
part-time and needs your recommendation. Your college has been
under external pressures, and those of conscience, to increase the
number of minority staff. Do you think of the interests of the college or
of this young man's personal future as you visit with him? You know
that you can make him feel obligated to stay if you try.

Case 46 *Passing on Personal Observations*

A. You are a new president undergoing orientation with the
outgoing president. The outgoing president frequently gives you personal opinions of faculty, staff, and families although you have not
requested this briefing. Do you listen without comment, keeping an
open mind; or, do you tactfully suggest that you would rather not
know these things?

B. You are an outgoing president, moving on to a desired assignment elsewhere. There are some pitfalls to be avoided in dealing with
certain faculty members, and some successful techniques that work
with given individuals. Do you share these with the incoming president, or do you allow him to make mistakes and/or discover these for
himself?

C. You are a new president. You find that there a few faculty
members who are only too willing to share their personal observations
of others in order to help you along. What is your stance on this? What
if the helpful person is the personal secretary which you have inher-
ited and who seems to be genuinely motivated? What if he or she is a
vice president?

Case 47 *Budget Surplus*

It has been your custom to carry over a surplus of funds into the
new fiscal year. This is your college's reserve. It is no secret, and you
have explained your reasons for this in faculty meetings before. You
consider it good business practice, and most tenured faculty and the

governing board accept it. A delegation of two newer faculty comes to your office stating a contention that such surpluses should be put into salary raises for the faculty. What is your response?

Case 48 *Changing Facilities Plan*

You are new as a president. The college has a facilities plan. You are not sure how it was developed but several administrators and faculty seem knowledgeable about it. It was approved by the governing board a year or so earlier. Several faculty and one or two administrators talk with you about it individually. Each of these has some different notion of what is needed most at the college, and these are all different from the existing facilities plan. You are not yet sure about priorities of your own. Your college now comes into a million dollars in capital funds of a non-fiscal (continuing) nature. What do you do?

Case 49 *Mixed-Sex Dormitories*

A. The student government leaders come to you with a roughly sketched proposal for open, unlimited visitation in college dormitories. Your student personnel deans are adamantly opposed to this idea. They tell you that a lot of students do not want this invasion of their privacy in residence halls. You are quite sure that there will be strong parent opposition (and removal of students from dorms), and you know that your conservative governing board will never accept such a policy. How do you respond?

B. The student government leaders come to you with a proposal for a mixed-sex dormitory. All the conditions above tend to apply, except that the student personnel deans have noted that one dormitory yields itself architecturally to division by living areas with a common lounge. They are in the mood for compromise. How do you work with this issue?

Case 50 *Revise Internal Governance System*

A. The chair of the committee on faculty welfare matters comes to your office with a proposal from the committee to restudy the internal governance system at the college which was devised several years earlier with your participation and adopted by both faculty and regents. There are a couple of features that you might like to change, but you suspect that some faculty may want to change features which are basic to your administrative philosophy. How do you respond?

B. You are a new president in your first year. The faculty proposal mentioned above comes to your office. At this point you have not had adequate time to observe and experience the system in place. It appears to be reasonably sound, although there are a couple of confusing features. How do you respond?

Case 51 *Hiring a Friend*

There is a teaching vacancy in one of the academic departments. The chairperson has a friend that he would like to employ and recommends this person. You explain that a personnel search must take place prior to any decision. After the position is advertised and resumes received, the chair again recommends the friend. You are acquainted with the recommended person and regard her as friendly and professional. She may fit in well and perform adequately, but you and the dean do not believe that this person is as well qualified academically on paper as several others in the applicant pool. How do you respond?

Case 52 *Religious Conflict*

The division chairpersons and the dean have made up the evening class schedule. One faculty member comes to the president's office complaining that he regularly attends church services on Wednesday evening, the time that his night class is scheduled. He has spoken to the chairperson and dean, and they reportedly have shown no regard for his religious practices. On checking with the dean, it seems significant that this class be offered on that evening, and it is his turn to teach a night class. They think he is overly rigid about his religion and just does not want to teach at night. What is your approach?

Case 53 *Participation in Commencement*

You are a new president. You understand that participation in commencement exercises by faculty personnel has been minimal. You want to stress the importance of the associate degree to students and the public. You believe that the pageantry of commencement helps do this. One reason (or excuse) heard for nonparticipation is the cost of renting of academic costumes. Do you require participation? What is your solution?

Case 54 *Attendance at College Activities*

Less than a third of the faculty attend athletic contests with any regularity. An even smaller proportion attend music, drama, fine arts, and lyceum events. Student attendance is similarly proportioned. You believe that the activities program adds vitality to the campus life, you invest resources in these areas, and you think that faculty need to take the lead. How do you approach this problem?

Case 55 *New Budget System*

You are the president of a small, rural, state junior college. Your curriculum provides for heavy enrollments in expensive computer and health occupation fields. The state coordinating board (or legislative committee) is considering a new budgeting system. This system involves peer comparisons, with the notion of bringing state institutions up to the average per student expenditures in like-type colleges. The university peer group appears "aspirant" in nature, including the best in the land, while others are not. Also, large two-year colleges are mixed with small ones to arrive at an average per student expenditure (total dollars divided by total FTE students by state) for your peer group. Inside the state, each junior college is to be budgeted according the same per student figure derived from this process. What are your objections to this procedure, if any? Why?

Case 56 *Accrediting Team Representation*

You are the president of a small, rural junior college in the conservative heartland. Due for a periodic accreditation evaluation visit, you are assigned a team of five persons. One teaches higher education classes in a prestigious university, and the other four are liberal arts faculty members from unionized metropolitan community colleges. Is this a concern? Why? What do you do?

BIBLIOGRAPHY & SUGGESTED READINGS

Alexander, K., & Solomon, E. S. *College and University Law*. The Michie Company, Charlottesville, VA, 1972.

Aylesworth, L. L. "College Experiences and Problems of Rural and Small Town Students," *Journal of College Student Personnel*, (May, 1976) 236-242

Baker, G. A., Roueche, J. E. & Rose, R. R. "Transformational Leaders in the Community College," *Community, Technical, and Junior College Journal*, 58 (June, 1988) 36-41.

Baldridge, V. & Deal, T. "The Basics of Change in Educational Organizations," *The Dynamics of Organizational Change in Education*, (Baldridge and Deal, Eds.). McCuthan Press, Berkley CA, 1982, 1-12.

Benezet, L. T. "Do Presidents Make a Difference?" *Educational Record*, 63 (Fall, 1982) 11-13.

Benezet, L. T., Katz, J. & Magnussion, F. W. *Style and Substance: Leadership and the College Presidency*. American Council on Education, Washington, DC, 1981.

Boggs, G. R. "Pathways to the Presidency," *Community, Technical, and Junior College Journal*, 59 (June, 1989) 41-43.

Cameron, K.S. "Organizational Adaptation and Higher Education," *Journal of Higher Education*, 55 (May, 1984) 36-40.

Carter, E. "Assessing Community College Effectiveness," *Community, Technical, and Junior College Journal*, 60 (August, 1989) 57-59.

Clodius, J. & McGrath, D. S. *The President's Spouse: Volunteer or Volunteered?* National Association of State Universities and Land Grant Colleges, Washington, DC, 1984.

Cloud, R. C. "Thoughts on Stress and College Administration," *Community College Review*, 19 (Summer, 1991) 24-29.

Cohen, A. M. & Brawer, F. B.(Editors). *Handbook on Community College Administration*. Jossey-Bass, San Francisco, CA, 1993.

Conrad, C., "A Grounded Theory of Academic Change," *Sociology of Education*, 51 (April, 1978) 101-112.

Deegan, W. L. & Tillery, D. *Renewing the American Community College.* Jossey-Bass, San Francisco, CA, 1985.

Duncan, A. H. & Harlacher, E. L. "The Twenty-First Century Executive Leader," *Community College Review*, 18 (Spring, 1991) 39-47.

Fisher, J. L. *The Power of the Presidency.* American Council on Education/Macmillan, New York, NY, 1984.

Gunn, B. "Reformation in the Administration of Higher Education," *College Student Journal*, (Fall, 1984) 1-35

Hall, G. L. *100,000 and Under.* AACJC monograph series, Washington, DC, 1969

Hall, R. A. & Alfred, R. L. "Applied Research on Leadership in Community Colleges," *Community College Review*, 12 (Spring, 1985) 36-41.

Hammons, J. O. & Keller, L. "Competencies and Personal Characteristics of Future Community College Presidents," *Community College Review*, 18 (Winter, 1990) 34-41.

Heimer, M., Heck, J. C. & Wattenbarger, J. L. "Patterns of Adjustment: What Happens to Community College Presidents Following Retirement," *Community, Technical, and Junior College Journal*, 58 (June, 1988) 24-28.

Horvath, R. J. "I Dare You," *Community, Technical, and Junior College Journal*, 58 (June, 1988) 28-32.

Hough, W. "Power and Influence in the Change Process," *Educational Leadership*, 36 (1978) 55-59.

Kaiser, M. G. & Greer, D. "Legal Aspects of Personnel Management in Higher Education," *New Directions for Community Colleges*, 16-2 (Summer, 1988) 61-70.

Kaplin, W. A. *The Law of Higher Education.* Jossey-Bass, San Francisco, CA, 1985.

Kauffman, J. F. *At the Pleasure of the Board: The Service of the College and University President.* American Council on Education/Macmillan, New York, NY, 1980.

Kerr, C. *Presidents Make a Difference.* Association of Governing Boards, Washington, DC, 1984.

Kerr, C. & Gade, M. L. *The Many Lives of Academic Presidents.* Association of Governing Boards, Washington, DC, 1986.

Lindquist, J. "Political Linkages," *Journal of Higher Education*, 45 (May, 1974) 323-340.

Magelli, P. J. "Leadership for the Future," *Community, Technical, and Junior College Journal*, 60 (April, 1990) 48-51.

Meardy, W. H. "A Shot in the Foot: Advice for Presidential Applicants," *ACCT Advisor*, 18 (March, 1987) 2-3.

McCurry, D. "Hogwash: The Community College in the Rural Crisis," *Community College Frontiers*, 3 (Spring, 1975) 4-7

McLeod, C., Marshall, W. & Carter, R. A. "The Measure of Quality in Two-Year Colleges," *Community College Review*, 13 (Spring, 1986) 14-21.

Miller, R. I. & Holzapfel, E. W. (Editors). *Issues in Personnel Management*. New Directions for Community Colleges, No. 62, 16-2 (Summer, 1988), Jossey-Bass, San Francisco, CA, 1988.

Nolan, M. F. "The Rural Redevelopment Act: A Skeptical View," *Rural Sociology*, 39 (Winter, 1974) 536-543.

Pfeffer, J. "Management as Symbolic Action," *Research in Organizational Behavior* (Cummings, Ed.). JAI Press, Greenwich, CT, 1981, 1-52.

Pondy, L.R. "Leadership is a Language Game," *Leadership: Where Else Can We Go?* (McCall, Ed.). Duke University Press, Durham, NC, 1978, 87-99.

Puyear, D. E., Perkins, J. R.& Vaughan G. B. "Pathway to the Presidency," *Community, Technical, and Junior College Journal*, 60 (April, 1990) 33-35.

Roe, M. A. & Baker, G. A. "The Development of Future Community College Leaders," *Community College Review*, 16 (Spring, 1989) 5-16.

Rogers, G. & Steinhoff, C. "Preparing Students for Minimum Competency Testing," *Community College Review*, 18 (Spring, 1991) 33-39.

Seldin, P. *Evaluating and Developing Administrative Performance: A Practical Guide for Academic Leaders*. Jossey-Bass, San Francisco, CA, 1988.

Sullins, W. R. & Atwell, C. A. "The Role of the Small Rural Community College in Providing Access," *Community College Review*, 13 (Spring, 1986) 45-51.

Thrash, P. "Outcomes Evaluation in the Accreditation Process," *NCA Quarterly*, 61 (Spring, 1989) 481-490.

Tucker, A. & Bryan, R. A. *The Academic Dean: Dove, Dragon, and Diplomat 2/e*. American Council on Education/Macmillan, New York, NY, 1991.

Vaughan, G. B. "Learning in Transit at Mountain Empire," *Community and Junior College Journal*, 44 (June, 1974) 33-35.

Vaughan, G. B. *The Community College Presidency*. American Council on Education/Macmillan, New York, NY, 1986.

Vaughan, G. B. "Scholarship in Community Colleges: The Path to Respect," *Educational Record*, 69 (Spring, 1988) 26-31.

Vaughan, G. B. *The Presidential Team: Perspectives on the Role of the Spouse of a Community College President*. AACJC, Washington, DC, 1987.

Vaughan, G. B. *Leadership in Transition: The Community College Presidency*. American Council on Education/Macmillan, New York, NY, 1989.

Vaughan, G. B. & Templin, R. G. "Value Added: Measuring Community College Effectiveness," *Community, Technical, and Junior College Journal*, 59 (April, 1989) 38-45.

Vaughan, G. B. "Female Community College Presidents," *Community College Review*, 17 (Fall, 1989) 20-26.

Vineyard, E. E. "The Invisible Wall," *Report of the Task Force on Small/Rural Community Colleges*, AACJC, Washington, DC, 1978.

Vineyard, E. E. "The Rural Community College." *Community College Review*, 6 (Winter, 1979) 29-45.

Vineyard, E. E. "Has Academic Liberalism Outlived Its Usefulness?" *College and University Business*, (March, 1969) 38-42.

Vineyard, E. E. "The General Education Component," *Community and Junior College Journal*, 48 (May, 1978) 24-25.

Vineyard, E. E. "Academic Strength Through Personnel Practices," *Handbook on Community College Administration*, (Cohen and Brawer, Editors). Jossey-Bass, San Francisco, CA, 1993.

Vineyard, E. R. "A Comparison of Views Toward Change and Proposals for Reform in Higher Education." Unpublished Doctoral Dissertation, Oklahoma State University, Stillwater, OK, 1989.

Volkwein, J. F. "Campus Autonomy and Its Relationship to Measures of University Quality," *Journal of Higher Education*, (September, 1986) 510-527.

Weber, J. "Assessment and Placement: A Review of the Research," *Community College Review*, 13 (Winter, 1986) 21-32.

Welker, W. F. & Morgan, S. D. "Beyond What the Literature Says on Institutional Effectiveness in Community Colleges," *Community College Review*, 19 (Fall, 1991) 25-31.

Whisnant, W. T. "The Presidential Image: Key to Effective Leadership," *Community College Review*, 17 (Spring, 1990) 10-14.

INDEX